# ANCIENT SITES OF HAWAI'I

Archaeological Places of Interest on the Big Island

Published by Mutual Publishing

First Printing, November 1996
Second Printing, August 1998
1 2 3 4 5 6 7 8 9

Softcover
ISBN 1-56647-200-8

Design, illustrations and photography by Van James

Mutual Publishing
1215 Center Street, Suite 210
Honolulu, Hawaii 96816
Telephone (808) 732-1709
Fax (808) 734-4094
e-mail: mutual@lava.net

Printed in Korea

# ANCIENT SITES OF HAWAI'I

Archaeological Places of Interest on the Big Island

*Van James*

Mutual Publishing

Dedicated to my wife Bonnie

and

*nā ēwē hānau o ka ʻāina*

# CONTENTS

# FOREWORD

In ancient times, the sacred places of Hawai'i, or *wahi pana* of Hawai'i, were treated with great reverence and deference. These places possess spiritual power, *mana*, but the designation *wahi pana* means much more than just a sacred geographical spot. In Hawaiian culture, the idea of "place" itself holds deep meaning.

As a native Hawaiian, a place tells me who I am and who my extended family is. A place gives me my history, the history of my clan, and the history of my people. I am able to look at a place and tie in human events that affect me and my loved ones. A place gives me a feeling of stability and of belonging to my family, those living and dead. A place gives me a sense of well-being and of acceptance of all who have experienced that place.

The gods and their disciples specified places that were sacred. The inventory of sacred places in Hawai'i includes the dwelling places of the gods, the dwelling places of venerable disciples, temples, and shrines, as well as selected observation points, cliffs, mounds, mountains, weather phenomena, forests, and volcanoes. As my ancestral religion functions through a hierarchy of gods, practices, and lore, the *wahi pana*, too, are hierarchical. A *wahi pana* favored by a dominant god or a high-status disciple is inherently more remarkable than one favored by a lesser god or being. The great god Kū is associated with the *luakini heiau*, or temple, while the lesser manifestation of Kū known as Kū'ula is associated with a lower order of fishing shrine.

The gods defined many *wahi pana*, but so did individuals, events, and functions. The south point of Hawai'i island, Ka Lae, is a *wahi pana* of long-distance voyaging and offshore fishing. Ka Lae served as a navigational reference for oceanic travel between Hawai'i and southern Polynesia, and priests communed there to use its *mana* in planning.

Though *wahi pana* are normally associated with geographical areas, this is not always so. For instance, Paliuli, a divine place of much spiritual presence, cannot be found with a map or jungle guide. Paliuli is discoverable only if one's mind and soul are ready to receive this *wahi pana* in the uplands of Hilo. Conversely, the water hole Palehemo, in the district of Ka'ū gained spiritual status through functional use over many generations.

I use the *wahi pana* in my practice of *pono,* or righteousness, which results in an increase in my *mana. Wahi pana* rituals are usually performed when no uninvited guests are present; therefore, night and early morning ceremonies are typical. The rituals involve prayers, offerings, and conversations with deities. The rituals are closed because the ignorant often offend and desecrate rather than honor. Yet I have at times seen even foreigners, who have only read about the goddess Pele, bring acceptable offerings, such as food and foliage. The difference, of course, lies in individual sensitivity, thoughtfulness, and humility. These are the qualities needed to fully benefit from any *wahi pana.*

Visitors are of many different philosophical and spiritual persuasions but whatever the visitor's mind set it is vital that the visitor validate the native Hawaiian culture. In the case of *wahi pana,* the native Hawaiian culture's sacred places, one should give due respect. For the tourist or the resident who is not a practitioner, a minimal duty should be that one has the intent of doing no harm to the site. One should prevent harm to the *wahi pana.* One should take a moment to reflect upon the wonder that is associated with the *wahi pana.* One should not give any offering (never leave a rock covered with a ti leaf). One should not disturb or take any souvenir rocks or other material because such an action affects one's spiritual safety. Neither should one leave a spiritual or personal object at a *wahi pana* since that action also affects one's spiritual safety.

If the visitor feels spiritually compelled to connect with a *wahi pana* then one should offer a *ho'okupu.* One of the *ho'okupu* of highest value in the native Hawaiian culture is not an offering of fruits or vegetables or foliage; neither is it an offering of a fish or a whale's tooth or a family heirloom; rather it is one's word! One's commitment! One's promise! One's sincere oath to pay deference to and uphold the physical and spiritual values of the culture! One's word is the *ho'okupu* of choice!

These guidelines are easily followed. Also easily followed is Van James's guide to the sites and *wahi pana* of Hawai'i island. This text mirrors the cautions of the native Hawaiian but also celebrates the joy that the native Hawaiian has toward the sacred sites. There are some forbidden sites that are not to be visited but Van James has thoughtfully excluded them. The book contains the native Hawaiian values of functionality, seeking knowledge, and enjoying adventure. Whether *kama'āina* or *malihini* or native Hawaiian, we can all use and delight in this work.

—Edward L.H. Kanahele
Panaewa, Hawai'i

# INTRODUCTION

One of the reasons for this guidebook on ancient sites of Hawai'i is to encourage not only visitors to Hawai'i but especially *malihini* (newcomers) and *kama'āina* (children of the land) to familiarize themselves with the ancient legacy of this unique place in the Pacific. Hawaiian prehistory is an important chapter in the history of humanity, and the sites illustrating this cultural period should be accessible so that they can be more fully appreciated and more clearly understood as markers of the present in our journey from past to future.

An attempt has been made with this book to bring together introductory background material concerning various Big Island sites. Differing opinions among scholars and researchers, as well as oral traditions and legends, have been presented wherever possible. Still, this work is anything but an exhaustive study. Only a few of the island's numerous sites are mentioned here. The intention is simply to introduce and guide readers to sites that are generally known and easily accessible. In some cases, permission or an entrance fee is required, but in all cases the sites listed here are open to interested visitors. Be aware that site circumstances may have changed since the writing of this book.

It is important that more people find that archaeology, ancient art, myths and legends, and even place names can add rich and enlivening dimensions to their understanding of Hawai'i. Reading cannot replace the experience of standing at a site and encountering with all one's senses the way a natural formation or a human construction is set within the elements. A *heiau* (temple) carefully placed on a mountain ridge, or a *pōhaku* (stone) declaring its commitment to a particular location can only be experienced through a visit to the site itself. The intention of a petroglyph image or the structure and mood created by a fishpond read differently in nature than in print because their art and mystery are not yet trapped and interpreted by the intellect.

Most of the sites included in this book are sacred to the native Hawaiian people. The sites and their surroundings should be treated with reverence and respect; nothing should be removed or altered. It is also important that visitors leave nothing that could have an impact on the monument or the environment. In the case of *heiau*, which are sometimes burial places, rock walls and platforms should not be climbed or crossed unless an obvious path is provided.

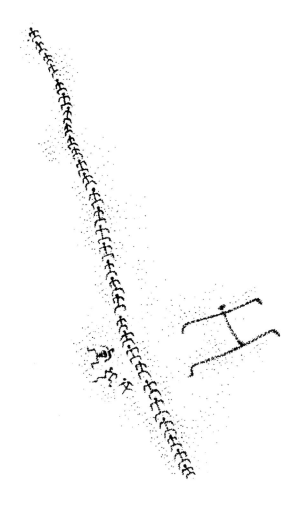

A column of twenty-nine petroglyph figures at Puakō, Kohala, could be marching warriors flanked by *ali'i* figures or an indication of a family's lineage.

When first visiting a site, view it from a distance, considering the immediate impression it has upon you. Proceed up to and gradually move around the site, noting its size, shape, material, and placement in the surroundings. Often only a pile of rocks is to be seen. Note the angle of the light and how the shadows fall. See how the landscape embraces the site. Consider the vegetation growing nearby. (Remember that a forested area may have been treeless a century or two ago, and what is now a clearing may have been overgrown.) Take in the views from various directions at the site. Not least of all, be conscious of your feelings as you actively appreciate the site.

It is sad to report that many ancient sites on Hawai'i have been destroyed by nature, development, and vandalism, but new sites are continually being discovered and interest in saving ancient sites is growing. This book is intended to promote appreciation and preservation of the ancient sites of Hawai'i.

—Van James
Honolulu, Hawai'i

## ACKNOWLEDGMENTS

I would like to thank a number of people for helping me with the material for *Ancient Sites of Hawai'i*. They include Dan Akaka, Patty Belcher, Patty Edwards, Mary Endel, Victoria Gold, Bonnie Goodell, Dan Kraus, Elizabeth Lee, Robin Lee, Kelly Loo, Clint and Audrey Marantz, Dot and George Mason, Ellen and Sus Nakagawa, Barry Nakamura, Bonnie Ozaki, Barbara Pope, Tia Reber, Jeff Schwartz, Richard Swingle, Peter Wind, Leka of Keauhou Beach Hotel, Moana of King Kamehameha Hotel, Momi Sheehan and Lani Opunui Ancheta of Kona Village Resort, Momi Lum, Paul Daulquist and the staff of the Lyman Museum, David Del Rocco and the 'Aina Haina Public Library, Ross Cordey and Tom Dye of the State Preservation Division of the Department of Land and Natural Resources, Martha Yent of State Parks, Paul Andrade, Irving Brock, David van Nest, and Laura Carter of the National Park Service, the staffs of Bishop Museum Archive and Hilo Public Library, and the faculties of Mālamalama School and the Honolulu Waldorf School.

I want especially to acknowledge Edward Kanahele, whose Foreword sets the proper conditions for visiting the ancient sites of Hawai'i. Mahalo to David Eyre for his help with the Hawaiian language and his contribution on Hawaiian Pronunciation. My sincere thanks to Cammy Dol for editing the original manuscript. Many thanks also to Jane Hopkins and Mutual Publishing for their timely and professional work on this edition. I would also like to thank Bishop Museum for its kind permission to reprint some excerpts from *Ancient Sites of O'ahu* and for the use of numerous *kapa* designs from its collection.

# HOW TO USE THIS BOOK

This guidebook begins with a brief survey of ancient Hawaiian culture and a description of the five major types of sites to be found on the island of Hawai'i. A map of Hawai'i showing site locations appears on page 42 and thirty of the island's most accessible ancient sites, along with descriptions, photographs, and detailed area maps, are presented in the second half of the book.

The sites are grouped into six traditional districts of the Big Island: Hilo, Puna, Ka'ū, Kona, Kohala, and Hāmākua, all of which still serve as present-day land divisions. (Hilo, Kona, and Kohala have not been divided here into north and south districts.) The sites of some districts can be viewed in one day of touring. In some cases, the sites of two or more districts can be combined into one trip. However, the Kona and Kohala coasts have such a wealth of archaeological resources that several days would be necessary to view the ancient sites of these districts adequately.

If you are visiting Hawai'i, are unfamiliar with the Big Island, and have little time to explore, you might read the site descriptions first and then simply pick and choose those you wish to see. "Appendix A: Selected Sites for Visitors" offers some suggestions for first-time explorers.

The local *kama'āina* (child of the land) site-seer has the advantage of time and can also make use of the "pick- and-choose" approach. Read the site descriptions and arrange your excursions as time and circumstances permit.

If you are interested in particular kinds of sites, such as petroglyphs, just consult the list at the end of the "Types of Sites" chapter, then find your selection by title in the "Site Locations" section.

Those interested in further information on ancient sites can consult the "Bibliography" at the back of the book. Following each site description in the text, you will find groups of numbers in parentheses. The first number indicates a title in the

"Bibliography" and the second number refers to the pages in that book wherein the site is discussed.

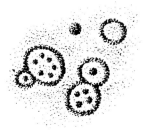

Most petroglyph images are of circles and dots like these found at Pu'u Loa (Site II.9 page 66) Puna. The dot, a *puka* or *lua* (hole), was, according to tradition, a receptacle for a newborn child's *piko* (umbilical cord stump). The dot within a circle is thought to be for the first-born of an *ali'i* family, and the circle alone is thought to be an *'umeha* (calabash) awaiting the *piko* of a new child.

## The Ancient Hawaiians

Like most indigenous peoples, the ancient Hawaiians felt a deep connection with nature. They experienced the forces that caused thunder and lightning or created sunshine and rainbows to be the same elemental forces that allowed them to stand, to walk, and to chant. These natural forces were so powerful and so alive to the Hawaiians that they were called by name and recognized as beings. Thus, an entire pantheon of gods, goddesses, and demigods was associated with the elements of water, snow, clouds, and fire, and dwelt in fish, animals, plants, and other natural phenomena. The gods Kū, Kāne, Lono, the goddess Pele, and the demigod Māui are just a few of the supernatural beings remembered today in Hawai'i.

The ancient Hawaiian fisherman, *kalo* (taro) farmer, canoe builder, and *kapa* or cloth maker, were in constant converse with nature and, thereby, in regular discourse with the gods. The soil, stones, plants, wood, wind, clouds, and light all expressed a meaning-filled content. For this reason, the ancient Hawaiians were sensitive to and revered the world around them. By reading the "Book of Nature," Hawaiians developed effective medical arts based entirely on natural remedies. Their knowledge also enabled them to develop and manage fishponds, some of the most advanced aquaculture in the Pacific. This is not to say that the ancient Hawaiians had a perfect society without injustice, illness, or environmental destruction. In some respects, however, their culture exemplified how a human community could be self-sufficient and enjoy a harmonious and mutually beneficial relationship with nature.

## Myths and Legends

*"These are my gods, whom I worship. Whether I do right or wrong I do not know. But I follow my faith, which cannot be wicked, as it commands me never to do wrong."*
—Kamehameha I

This intimate relationship to nature was expressed in lively, imaginative stories and passed on from one generation to the next in the form of chants, or *ka'ao* and *mo'olelo*. Myths related accounts of the major gods and goddesses, while legends passed on the more localized tales into which much of the cultural history of old Hawai'i was woven. In addition to the myths and legends, oral tradition presented factual or historic accounts from the more recent past. Meaning, morality, and spiritual values were an integral part of the mythological, legendary, and traditional histories. Such accounts demonstrated how the world arose as a result of the creative spirit, how physical objects and facts were the results of godly deeds. In this sense, Pele, the volcano goddess, was seen as the inspirer of imagemaking in Hawai'i, perhaps because of the unending form possibilities that can be found in lava rock structures. The fiery, creative spirit Pele thus establishes herself as the first sculptor.

## The *Kapu* System

*Mālama o pā 'oe.*
Be careful lest the result be disastrous to you.

*[Watch your step lest evil attach itself to you.*
*A warning not to break a kapu.]*
—Hawaiian saying (35/231)

The social order of old Hawai'i rested on the principle of *mana*, the spiritual power that all things possess to a greater or lesser degree. Stones, plants, animals, people, and the gods all possess this vital force, according to the Hawaiians. In order to protect and revere this sacred *mana*, laws or *kapu* were established. These *kapu* set down strict societal "do's and don't's" and the transgressor often paid with his or her life. Examples of important *kapu* were fishing out of season, stepping on the chief's shadow, and eating bananas or pig if you were a woman. Acquittal was possible for a *kapu* breaker if he or she could reach a *pu'uhonua* (place of refuge) and be cleansed and exonerated of the misdeed by a *kahuna* (priest). In times of war, the *pu'uhonua* was especially important as a refuge for warriors and women and children whose side had been defeated in battle.

The *kapu* system, as it is understood today, primarily maintained the power and authority of the *ali'i*, or chiefly class, within the social order. It was also instrumental in defining traditional beliefs and preserving ancient knowledge and customs.

## The *Ali'i*

*He 'ehu wāwae no kalani.*
A trace of the heavenly one's footsteps.

*[The rain, the rainbow, and other signs seen when*
*a chief is abroad are tokens of his recognition by*
*the gods.]*
—Hawaiian saying (35/65)

The *ali'i*, or royal class, were at the pinnacle of the Hawaiian social order and *kapu* system. This highborn group possessed great *mana* and were therefore the rulers and leaders of the people. They were the heads of the community, the caretakers of their ancestors' memory, and the guardians of the gods on earth. Some ruled well, protecting their subjects from harm whenever possible; others ruled poorly, taking advantage of the *kapu* system and inflicting suffering for no apparent reason.

Kamehameha the Great (1758-1819) was perhaps the most powerful of the island chiefs and is believed by many to have been a wise and noble leader. An exceptional destiny was forecast for "the lonely one," who was born during the appearance of Halley's Comet. As a young man, he proved himself a fierce warrior in battle and, as another sign of his greatness, moved the legendary Naha stone in Hilo. His uncle, Chief Kalani'ōpu'u, appointed Kamehameha guardian of the family war god, Kūkā'ilimoku, "Kū the Land Grabber," and divided up the island of Hawai'i between his two sons, Kiwala'ō and Keōua, Kamehameha's cousins. Kamehameha gained the Kona and Kohala districts of Hawai'i by defeating his elder cousin, Kiwala'ō, at the Battle of Moku'ōhai in 1782. He gained control over the rest of the Big Island in 1791 when he invited Keōua to the dedication of Pu'ukoholā Heiau and then offered him as the sacrifice.

Kamehameha the Great (1758-1819) established the kingdom of Hawai'i by uniting all of the islands under his rule. He was born in the North Kohala district of the Big Island; his name means "the lonely one" or "the one alone." (Based on a sketch by Ludwig Choris, 1816.) Ka'ahumanu, the favorite wife of Kamehameha, served as regent of Hawai'i after the king's death in 1819 until her own death in 1832. She played an important part in the overthrow of the *kapu* system.

Kamehameha went on to conquer Maui, Moloka'i, and O'ahu by 1795. He reached an agreement with Kaua'i in 1810 that made Kamehameha ruler of all the Hawaiian Islands. As the first chief to unite all of the Hawaiian Islands, he was also the first king. Shortly after his death, the ancient *kapu* system collapsed when, in 1819, his favorite wife, Ka'ahumanu, his highborn wife, Keōpūolani, and his son, Liholiho (Kamehameha II), abolished the old laws as well as the traditional religious order.

## The Kāhuna

*Ko ke kahuna ha'i kupua.*
To the *kahuna* belongs the duty of declaring the revelations of the supernatural beings.
—Hawaiian saying (35/196)

Kamehameha I and other powerful chiefs had *kāhuna*, priests or specialists, who served as their advisors. These *kāhuna* were not only spiritual counselors but political advisors as well. Particularly skilled *kāhuna* often provided needed guidance and direction for the *ali'i*.

Hawaiian oral tradition speaks of Pā'ao, a light-skinned *kahuna* who came to the islands sometime between the tenth and thirteenth centuries from Kahiki. (Some sources suggest that Kahiki refers to Samoa, Tahiti, or the Society Islands while others point to the Marquesas or the Cook Islands as the place of origin of the early Hawaiians.) Arriving on the Big Island of Hawai'i, Pā'ao overthrew the harsh Big Island chief, Kamaiole, and sent for a suitable *ali'i* from his homeland to be installed as the new high chief. Pili Ka'ai'ea was brought to Hawai'i, establishing a new royal line that would lay the foundations for later rulers such as the Kamehameha lineage. A strong *kapu* system seems to have been emphasized at this time, along with the practice of human sacrifice. Pā'ao is also credited with encouraging the carving of wooden *ki'i*, or images, for religious purposes, and the building of more elaborate *heiau* (temples) than had previously been constructed.

*Kāhuna* were not always spiritual or political advisors. A *kahuna* was, in fact, anyone who was expert in a particular field. Doctors, artists, craftspersons, even master farmers and fishermen could be *kāhuna*. Long training was required of the apprentice *kahuna* before he or she gained the knowledge and discipline to become *kahuna lapa'au* (medical practioner), *kahuna kālai* (master carver), *kahuna hana 'upena* (master fishnetmaker), or *kahuna ho'oulu 'ai* (agricultural expert). Such skills were passed from one generation to another, from teacher to pupil, through hands-on repetitive practice, often from a young age. No texts, scores, or written notations helped the *haku mele* (master of chants and music) learn to recall and chant the thousands of lines of verse required to preserve the oral history. No compass, charts, or sextant aided the *kahuna ho'okele* (navigator), and yet by reading the size, shapes, and colors of clouds, wave movements, flights of birds, currents, and stars, this *kahuna* learned to guide his voyaging canoe over thousands of sea miles (an accomplishment doubted in the West until only recently). The disciplines developed by the *kahuna* class clearly demonstrate a civilization that, although not technically advanced in a modern sense, displayed a high achievement in cultural life and human capabilities.

## Ancient Sites

The *kāhuna*, the *ali'i*, and the commoners made appropriate offerings to their *'aumākua* (ancestral spirits) and their gods. For such worship, they erected sacred *pōhaku* (stones), shrines, and *heiau* (temples). These ancient Hawaiian religious sites, together with petroglyphs and the remnants of fishponds, are but the bare bones of a once-flourishing civilization. Yet these remains from the archaeological record, in conjunction with myths, legends, and traditional history, provide us with a glimpse into the rich cultural life of old Hawai'i.

Most of the sites listed in this book are at least several hundred years old. As dating methods improve and new sites are discovered, the accepted time of settlement of the Hawaiian Islands continues to recede. The latest estimates now point to about the second or third century A.D. However, neither dating techniques nor the archaeological reconstructions of ancient sites are exact or final, as conclusions are usually based on limited evidence. What we may consider true today is often not what many thought was true yesterday nor what may be seen as true tomorrow.

This introduction to the ancient sites of Hawai'i deals only with *heiau* (temples), *pōhaku* (stones), petroglyphs (stone engravings), caves, and fishponds of the Big Island. Other features mentioned only in passing include house sites, animal pens, walls, agricultural terraces, irrigation ditches, wells, salt pans, paths and roadways, *hōlua* (sled) ramps, and *pu'uhonua* (places of refuge). These latter features should not be considered of lesser importance for they all contribute to a more comprehensive understanding of ancient Hawaiian culture and the sacredness of place or *wahi pana*. (2; 5; 9; 11; 16; 17; 20; 21; 26; 29; 30; 46)

*E hiolo ana na kapu kahiko;*
*e hina ana na heiau me na lele;*
*e hui ana na moku;*
*he iho mai ana ka lani a e pi'i ana ka honua.*
The ancient *kapu* will be abolished;
the *heiau* and altars will fall;
the islands will be united;
the heavens will descend and the earth ascend.

{A prophecy uttered by Kapihe, a *kahuna* in Kamehameha's time. The last part of the saying means that chiefs will come down to humble positions and commoners rise to positions of honor.}

—Hawaiian saying (35/35)

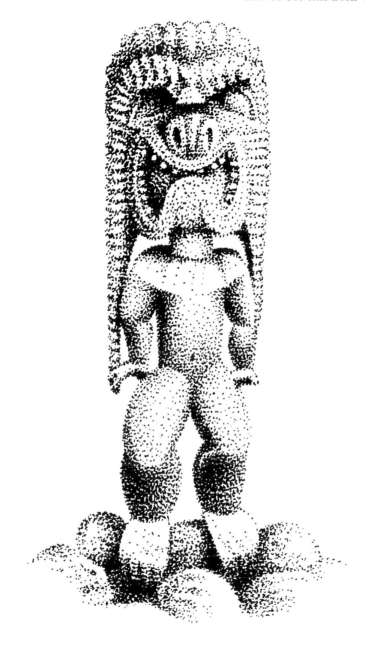

Kū, god of war, was usually depicted in a threatening pose with toothed grimace and flared nostrils. Such *akua ki'i*, carved wooden images, stood within and sometimes along the approach to *heiau* precincts. These images embodied the *mana* of certain gods and spirits; they were not taken to be the gods themselves, but rather to be channeling posts for divine powers. Few authentic *akua ki'i* survived the purging of the old religion initiated by the *ali'i* themselves in the early nineteenth century. This particular image is a late prehistoric Kona-style wood sculpture, and can be seen at the Bishop Museum in Honolulu.

# TYPES OF SITES

## *Heiau* (Temples) and Shrines

A *heiau* is a Hawaiian temple, a place of worship, offering, and/or sacrifice. It is not only one of the most enduring architectural forms from prehistoric Hawai'i but is also the most important architectural form from the perspective of Hawaiian religion. As with most ancient civilizations, the temple architecture well represents and expresses the culture. With an intense and immediate experience of the forces in nature and an intuitive relationship with their gods, the ancient Hawaiians looked to the *heiau* and their *kāhuna* (priests) for order, understanding, and guidance in the ways of the universe. This was the case even for practical everyday matters such as ascertaining the times for planting and harvesting, fishing and refraining from fishing, healing illness, and mending broken bones. Even giving thanks and being at peace with one's neighbors or going to war and taking another's life were connected with the role of the *kāhuna* and the *heiau*.

The *kahuna* was responsible to the people as a mediator between them and their gods. Many chiefs had a *kahuna* to consult, particularly on questions dealing with the maintenance of power, and the *heiau* was the main center for *kāhuna* activity.

According to oral tradition, Pā'ao was the first priest to bring from Kahiki a new religious impulse promoting and establishing a severe *kapu* (taboo) system. Some researchers believe that during his era, human sacrifice in connection with the worship of Kū, whose one aspect is god of war, superseded a more peaceful form of religious practice that centered on the god

Kāne. Pā'ao is said to be the *kahuna kuhikuhipu'uone*, or architect, behind the tenth-to-thirteenth-century Waha'ula Heiau as well as the Mo'okini Heiau on the island of Hawai'i, both of which were of the *luakini* (human sacrifice) type.

Lono, god of agriculture, fertility, and peace, was already revered in Hawai'i, along with Kū, at the time of the arrival of Pā'ao. Kāne, a god of freshwater sources, Kanaloa, god of the ocean, and numerous other gods were also worshipped at *heiau* throughout the islands.

The line of Big Island chiefs, leading down to Kamehameha I, seems to have stressed and ultimately spread a preference for Lono and the aggressive Kū over the other gods. Ahu'ena Heiau

in Kona is known to have honored an aggressive god of war as its central deity during its early period, but once Kamehameha had united the Hawaiian Islands, he rededicated the *heiau*, giving Lono prominence.

Only paramount chiefs, through their *kāhuna*, could consecrate *heiau* of the *luakini* type, where human sacrifices ensuring political power and preserving *mana* (spiritual power) were carried out. The preferred human sacrifice was a captive enemy, a warrior with much *mana*, *ali'i* (chiefs) having the greatest *mana*. A criminal was a second-class sacrifice, and the lowest grade was a *kauā* (outcast), a person considered to have little *mana* and to be capable of robbing *mana* from others.

Human sacrifice occurred late in the development of many ancient civilizations and it has been suggested that such practices may have been adopted in order to maintain a "fresh" connection to the spirit world at a time when spiritual vision was failing. Scholars today generally consider human sacrifice as a symbolic death and rebirth of the chief, for the purpose of maintaining and renewing the social order. Human sacrifice was the ultimate offering to the gods, petitioning them to preserve and revitalize society.

Although human sacrifice figured in only a small part of the religious practices of the ancient Hawaiians, the *heiau luakini* are nevertheless quite numerous and usually larger in size than other types of temples. This seems due, in part, to the tradition that only a few paramount chiefs held the privilege of establishing and using *luakini*, and that they did this to assert their power and demonstrate their prestige. (However, by the time temple functions were recorded, the term *luakini* had come to mean "religious place" and was applied even to Christian churches.) Besides Waha'ula and Mo'okini, another important *heiau luakini* on the Big Island is Pu'ukoholā Heiau in South Kohala, the last human sacrifice temple to be built in the islands.

All *heiau*, apart from the *luakini*, could be dedicated by lesser chiefs. Some of these other *heiau* were of the husbandry type, sometimes called Hale o Lono, where the promotion and increase of livestock and agriculture were fostered. The recently destroyed Moa Heiau at Kamoamoa in Volcanoes National Park was such a temple. The *heiau ho'oulu 'ai* were devoted to increasing the general food supply. *Heiau ma'o* were designed to promote rainfall and abundance in time of drought. Typical offerings at such *heiau* were pigs, bananas, and coconuts.

At a less common type of *heiau*, healers, known as *lapa'au*, were trained in the ancient art of medicine. Herbal remedies and spiritual healing were practiced at sacred sites throughout Hawai'i, and the surroundings of these *heiau* served as the natural pharmacy for plant remedies of all kinds. Keaīwa Heiau on O'ahu is the best-known site of this kind.

Many *heiau* were quickly constructed over a three-day period, used to fulfill a specific need, and then abandoned. Sites were reused only if the need arose.

No two *heiau* seem to have been constructed in the same way as far as ground plans are concerned. Though often built on a rectangular rock platform, some *heiau* were terraced or stepped with one or more levels, while others had walled enclosures. Some were square, some trapezoidal, and others were canoe-shaped or oval. Stone foundations are the only parts of these temples that we see today. Wooden fences often surrounded the temple precinct and thatched *hale* (houses) stood within the enclosure, but none

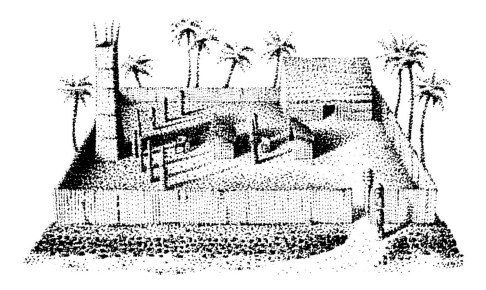

Typical features of the *luakini heiau* were, from left to right, the *'anu'u* (oracle tower), which was entered only by the *kāhuna; akua ki'i* (wooden images of the gods/ancestors); the *lele* (altar) for offerings; the *hale pahu* (drum house); more *akua ki'i;* the *hale wai ea* (house of the ceremonial *'aha* cord); the oven house; the *hale mana* (house of spiritual power) for the *ali'i;* and more images at the entrance of the precinct.

of these features has survived. At some sites, such as Ahu'ena Heiau in Kailua-Kona and Hale o Keawe Heiau at Pu'uhonua o Hōnaunau in South Kona, these perishable structures have been reconstructed.

One of the *hale* within the *heiau* precinct would have been the *hale mana* (place of spiritual power) or the house of the resident god. Sometimes a *hale pahu* (drum house), a *wai ea* (small house where incantations were invoked), and an oven house were also present. Wooden structures covered with *kapa*, or tapa cloth, were where the *kahuna* received visions or messages from the gods. Called the *ōpū* or the *'anu'u* tower, these vertical enclosures are also referred to as oracle towers and stood near the *lele* or altar. *Akua ki'i* (sacred wooden images of the gods) guarded the entrance to the compound and watched over the altar. Although graves have been found within *heiau* precincts, a *heiau* should not be thought of as a cemetery in the contemporary sense. Burials were possible aids for a *kahuna* in his practice as a mediator between this world and the other and were sometimes temporary until a more appropriate cave or burial site could be found.

Not a great deal is known about the actual *heiau* rituals as they were already being abandoned before foreign settlers arrived in the early nineteenth century. One source of information is Captain James Cook's journals, wherein he describes *heiau* ceremonies he observed during his visits to the Hawaiian Islands in the late eighteenth century.

Describing the human sacrifice at *heiau luakini*, Samuel Kamakau, one of the native Hawaiian authorities writing in the mid-nineteenth century, said the dead person was reddened over a fire and placed face down with its right arm over a pig offering and its left hand holding a bunch of bananas. The high chief, or *mō'ī*, then pierced the mouth of the dead man with a ceremonial hook called the *mānaiakalani*, and recited the following words:

> *E Kū, e Lono,*
> *E Kāne, e Kanaloa,*
> *E ola ia'u a kau i ka puaneane;*
> *E nānā i ke kipi 'āina,*
> *I ka lelemū o.*
> *'Āmama. Ua noa.*
> O Kū, o Lono,
> O Kāne and Kanaloa,

Give life to me until my old age;
Look at the rebel against the land,
He who was seized for sacrifice.
Finished. It is freed of the *kapu*. (20/130)

The *kahuna nui* also recited a prayer and those assembled listened for the sound of a bird, lizard, or rat, a sign that the sacrifice had been accepted.

A special type of sacred area was the *pu'uhonua*, a place of refuge and forgiveness for *kapu* breakers. Every island had several such protected areas for the absolution of lawbreakers. The most famous of these is Pu'uhonua o Hōnaunau in Kona, on the Big Island.

The smaller common places of worship were the *ko'a* (fishing shrines), roadside *ahu* (piled stone marker) and boundary shrines. These shrines were numerous throughout the islands and sometimes consisted of a single upright *pōhaku* (stone) or perhaps a rock structure the size of a small *heiau*. They might be dedicated to an *'aumakua* (family god) or one of the many lesser Hawaiian gods or goddesses.

*Ko'a* were an important type of small shrine and remained in use long after more formal *heiau* functions ceased in Hawai'i. Fishermen offered their first catches at such shrines, which were usually located near the water. Some *ko'a* were sacred to specific fish and, when at the water's edge, were known to attract certain species. A *ko'a* might be one or more stones, naturally situated or deliberately placed, often in an upright position and sometimes featured on a rectangular or oval rock platform or enclosure. Platforms of this kind, as well as many *heiau*, often contained bits of white branch coral, even when the sites were located a great distance from the ocean.

It is believed that family shrines dedicated to the *'aumākua* were an important part of every household. These shrines took the form of a single stone "idol," signifying the *akua*, or guardian spirit, or an altar made up of many stones. Sometimes a special thatched *hale* (house) was built to house the *akua*; otherwise, the *akua* stood in the common living quarters or just outside in the open.

Road shrines often marked the boundary between one *ahupua'a* (land division) or district and another. There, travelers may have made offerings for a safe journey or left district tax payments, as was the custom. Today it may be difficult to imagine that a shrine, a sacred site, could be as simple as a single *pōhaku*.

Please remember to respect all *heiau* and shrines just as you would a church, temple, or any other sacred monument. (7; 10; 12; 14; 31; 43; 46)

## *Heiau* Sites by Region

II      Wahaʻula Heiau

III      Kāneʻeleʻele Heiau (Punaluʻu Fishpond)
Kalalea Heiau

IV      Hale o Keawe (Puʻuhonua o Hōnaunau)
Āleʻaleʻa Heiau (Puʻuhonua o Hōnaunau)
Hikiau Heiau
Keʻekū Heiau (Keauhou)
Hāpaialiʻi Heiau (Keauhou)
Kapuanoni Heiau (Keauhou)
Kuʻemanu Heiau
Ahuʻena Heiau
Makaʻōpio Heiau (Kaloko-Honokōhau)
Puʻuoina Heiau (Kaloko-Honokōhau)
Hale o Lono (Kaloko-Honokōhau)

V      Puʻukoholā Heiau
Mailekini Heiau (Puʻukoholā)
Moʻokini Heiau

〉〉〉 〉〉〉 〉〉〉 ▬ 〉〉〉 〉〉〉 〉〉〉 ▬

## *Pōhaku* (Sacred Stones)

Many of the prominent stones and distinctive rock formations on Hawai'i are sacred sites. Many of these sites have their own names and are featured in myths and legends. According to tradition, some represent individuals transformed into stone, while others serve as dwelling places for specific spirit beings or gods. Ka Wa'a o Māui (Māui's Canoe) in the Wailuku River marks where the demigod Māui left his legendary outrigger canoe.

The *pōhaku*, whether it was a small *'ili'ili* (pebble) or a megalithic *pali* (cliff), played a very significant part in the life of ancient Hawai'i. The features of the land spoke to the early Hawaiians in an imaginative, pictorial language and, therefore, many rocks and stones possessed distinctive characters and were given individual names.

Gifts for the local deity were often left at *pōhaku* sites. Various forms of ancestral worship were also celebrated at these sites, especially when the stones also marked burial places. However, *pōhaku* did not serve merely as gravestones in a conventional sense; rather they were altar-like monuments indicating where an ancestor could be contacted. Some stones were used by the *kāhuna* during spiritual practices and others served as boundary markers for land divisions or districts. Seen in this way, a *pōhaku* stood in the landscape as a physical reminder of a spiritual threshold. These sites were places of rest and relaxation where one could commune with the god or the ancestor. In some cases, the ancient Hawaiians may have read *pōhaku* shadows, much like one reads a sundial, to measure the divisions of the year. King's Pillars at Cape Kumukahi in Puna is thought to be a site where *kāhuna* observed the sun's movements.

Still other *pōhaku* were known as *ko'a* (fishing shrines) and were used to locate favorite fishing grounds. The first catch of the day was left at the *ko'a* as an offering of thanks to the god or goddess. A *kū'ula* stone was generally a medium-sized stone housing a spirit helpful to fishermen. Often speaking through a dream, a *kū'ula* could direct a fisherman to the stone's location and then, if properly cared for, might reward the fisherman with good fishing and a healthy life. Kū'ula is also the name of an important fish-god. (*See* Kalalea Heiau, Site III.13 pg. 80.)

Some stones were named after the fish, animals, or objects that their shapes suggested. Called Pōhaku o Kāne, they were often used as household shrines. Jagged and porous stones were considered female, while smooth fine-grained stones were thought of as male. Usually, light stones were female and dark-colored ones male.

In ancient times, Hawaiians would leave fist-sized stones on top of ti leaf offerings in order to prevent the leaf from blowing away. The strictly modern practice of wrapping a specially chosen stone in a ti leaf has evolved from the older tradition. (37; 38; 40; 47)

> *He ola ka pōhaku.*
> There is life in the stone.
> —Hawaiian saying

## *Pōhaku* Sites by Region

I      Pōhaku o Kāloa ('Akaka Falls)
        Ka Wa'a o Māui
        Mo'o Kuna (Rainbow Falls)
        Naha and Pinao Pōhaku
        Mokuola

II     Kumukahi

III    Punalu'u
       Pōhakuwa'a Kauhi (Kalalea Heiau)
       Pōhakuokeau (Kalalea Heiau)

IV     Ka'ahumanu Stone (Pu'uhonua o Hōnaunau)
       Kamehameha III Birthplace
       Kanaio and 'Ulupalakua Pōhaku (Keauhou)

V      Stone Leaning Post (Pu'ukoholā Heiau)
       Pōhaku Holehole Kānaka (Mo'okini Heiau)
       Kamehameha Rock

This four-foot-tall *pōhaku* image represents the fish god,
Kaneihokala, and was recovered from Kawaihae, Kohala,
around 1900. A Hawaiian man was led to its buried
location by a dream. As part of the Queen Emma
Collection, the stone image is on permanent display at
the Bishop Museum.

## *Ki'i Pōhaku* (Petroglyphs)

Petroglyphs (petro = stone, glyph = writing) are pictures, and sometimes words or letters, carved into rock surfaces. The Hawaiian expression is *ki'i pōhaku*, meaning "images engraved in stone."

Hawaiian petroglyphs remained simple in style and imagery even after contact with European explorers, whalers, and missionaries. According to many authorities, Hawaiian petroglyphs did not have great cultic or religious significance beyond celebrating personal experiences or acknowledging the *'aumākua*. However, even with this more limited application in terms of religious expression, the creating of *ki'i pōhaku* was nevertheless a sacred craft as were the even more practical activities of weaving, wood carving, tattooing, and *kapa* or tapa cloth design. Stylized petroglyphs and the geometric designs of tattoos and tapa cloth represent some of the high points in the development of ancient Hawaiian two-dimensional visual arts.

Petroglyphs appear at well over 150 known sites in the Hawaiian Islands, and most of these sites are on the Big Island. The forms in these stone carvings are dots or cup marks (round indentations), circles, straight lines, wavy and curved lines, as well as simple stick figures denoting dogs, turtles, birds, pigs, crabs, and human beings. Early Hawaiians carved anthropomorphic (part human and part animal) figures as well as men on surfboards and canoe paddlers with paddles in hand. Sails and canoes are also represented. Post-contact petroglyphs depict western ships, horseback riders, and Hawaiian words (writing was introduced by nineteenth-century missionaries).

Four different techniques were used in creating petroglyphs. These varied with the sharpness of the artists' stone tools. Sharp adzes produced pecked and incised designs; duller tools created bruised and abraded designs. Metal tools were sometimes used in post-contact times.

Petroglyphs may indicate the boundary of a district or *ahupua'a* (land division). Many cultures worldwide have used markings of some kind at territorial borders. Ancient Hawaiian travelers were sometimes called upon to contribute to these sites by adding a stone or carving a figure as an offering.

Most of the Hawaiian petroglyphs were carved in smooth *pāhoehoe* lava rock, which provided a good surface for images. Some are even found in lava tube caves. However, *ki'i pōhaku* were also carved on the faces of large river boulders and on coralline sandstone ledges along the older geological coastal structures. All of the Big Island petroglyph sites mentioned here utilize the abundant lava rock surfaces.

Some of the Hawaiian rock art images are related to local mythology, while others may depict pre-contact and early historic events. An example of the latter are the so-called "marching warriors" at Puakō, believed to represent a particular war party or family lineage. Some petroglyphs are connected with a birth ritual where the umbilical cord stump of a newborn child is placed in a carved *puka* or *lua* (hole) and covered with a stone, as was done at Pu'u Loa (Site II.9, pg. 66). Of course, some images may have more than one meaning.

Hawaiian petroglyphs are not realistic renderings of nature but rather stylized, symbolic images of forces and beings. Figures are not depicted within a physical space: There is no ground line, no background, and, therefore, no foreshortening, perspective, or depth. The differing sizes of figures may indicate rank or social status as much as age and physical stature. Groupings of figures can be difficult to read as compositions because the various images may have been carved at different times and for different reasons. Where a cluster of figures occurs in a petroglyph field, the images at the center are generally understood to be the oldest, with later carvings taking whatever smooth surface area remains at the periphery.

The best time to view petroglyphs is in the early morning or late afternoon when the sun is low in the sky. Petroglyphs are often difficult to see at midday because little or no shadow is cast in the shallow carved image area. For the best photographic results, stand with your back to the sun.

People have tried various methods of reproducing petroglyphs over the years, but such techniques as rubbing and casting damage rock art. The only safe method of reproducing petroglyph designs is to photograph or make interpretive drawings of them. Never try to enhance petroglyph images by recarving or even chalking them. Avoid walking on image areas and stay on viewing platforms where they are provided. Please protect all petroglyph sites! (8; 27; 32)

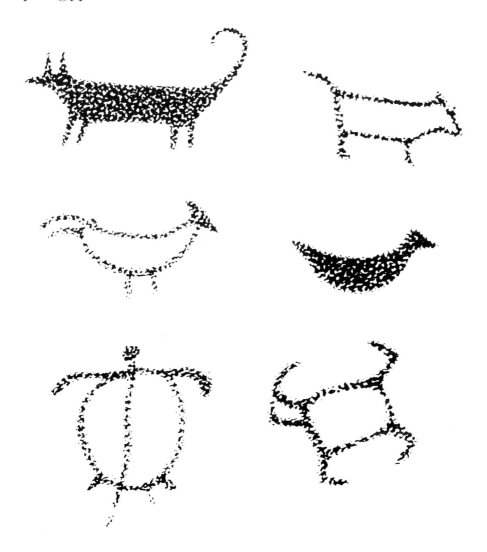

Some of the animals depicted at Puakō Petroglyph Preserve (Site V. 24, pg. 130) include a dog, chicken, turtle, pig, bird, and crab. Animals were often 'aumākua (guardian spirits) for Hawaiian families.

## Petroglyph Sites by Region

II      Pu'u Loa

III    Punalu'u

IV   Pu'uhonua o Hōnaunau
       Keauhou
       Ka'ūpūlehu

V      'Anaeho'omalu
       Kalāhuipua'a
       Puakō Petroglyphs

## Caves and Rock Shelters

The early Hawaiians used natural caves, lava tubes, and cliff overhangs as temporary shelters and places of refuge. Fishermen often took shelter from the weather in caves and bluff shelters close to the sea, as is indicated by archaeological evidence such as fishhooks and marine artifacts. Warriors used lava tube caves, some of which extended from the sea to the mountains, for hiding from enemies and for waiting in ambush. Such caves are noted in the traditions of the Kona district. Some caves were used as temporary homes; still others served as dwelling places of one or more gods and thus were *kapu* (taboo).

Burial caves were also *kapu*. They were fairly numerous and were used by *ali'i* (royalty) and commoners alike. Such caves provided ideal sites for laying the dead to rest and for seeking communion with ancestral spirits: Caves offer a place withdrawn from the outer world, an inner space, quiet, dark, and protected.

In some Hawaiian caves, the bones of the dead were placed in canoes meant to carry them on the voyage into the next world.

Most of the archaeologically important caves and lava tubes of Hawai'i are not included here as site locations because of the need to protect them. Many of these sites have not been excavated and others are on private land that should not be trespassed. Most important of all, many of these caves are the sacred resting places of native Hawaiians and should not be disturbed or violated. State law protects all Hawaiian burial sites.

The only accessible cave shelters open to the public listed here are Waiūohina Lava Tube, part of Pu'uhonua o Hōnaunau National Historic Park (Site IV.14, pg. 89), and a shelter cave at Kalāhuipua'a in Kohala. These sites have been stabilized and are part of interpretive preserves with hiking trails (pg. 126). Kaūmana Caves in Hilo and Thurston Lava Tube in Puna are also accessible but have no known archaeological or cultural significance as they are the result of historic lava flows.

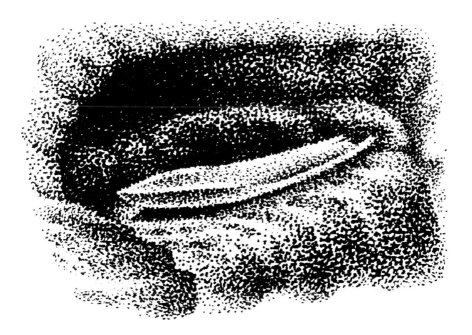

Some burials were committed to canoes for the soul's journey into the other world after death. The canoe and remains would be secretly placed in caves or rock shelters. Such sites are *kapu* and strictly off-limits to visitors.

*'A'ohe e nalo ka iwi o ke ali'i 'ino,*
*o ko ke ali'i maika'i ke nalo.*
The bones of an evil chief will not be concealed,
but the bones of a good chief will.

*[When an evil chief died, the people did not take*
*the trouble to conceal his bones.]*
—Hawaiian saying (35/17)

## Caves and Rock Shelters by Region

IV     Waiūohina Lava Tube (Pu'uhonua o Hōnaunau)

V      Kalāhuipua'a

## Fishponds

Fishing was one of the most important ancient Hawaiian livelihoods. Besides shoreline fishing along the rugged coast and open-sea fishing from canoes, the Hawaiians developed a very sophisticated aquaculture system using fishponds. Though many ponds have been destroyed and only a very few are still operational, in recent years a lively interest in rediscovering, restoring, and developing this ancient Hawaiian industry has occured.

Hawaiian fishponds are unique in their design and construction. Nowhere else in the Pacific has such an efficient, practical, and productive system of aquaculture developed. Evidence exists that fishponds were in use around 1200 A.D., which suggests their origin and development must have been even earlier.

Most fishponds contained saltwater or brackish water, but there were also freshwater ponds fed by streams and springs. Ponds had lanes or causeways to allow water in and out, and often *mākāhā* (wooden sluice gates) were employed. The *mākāhā* was designed to let small fish in to feed but to prevent them, once well fed and fat, from getting out. *'Anae* (mullet), *awa* (milkfish), and *āholehole* (silver perch) were commonly stocked in Hawaiian fishponds.

There are five different types of fishponds: *Loko 'ume iki, loko kuapā, loko pu'uone, loko wai,* and *loko i'a kalo.*

The *loko 'ume iki* is a large walled fishtrap as opposed to an actual pond. Built out in the ocean along the reef, *loko 'ume iki* usually had several openings leading into or out of the enclosure. The fish would then be netted from the openings. *'Ume iki* means to "draw" or "attract" "a little," which is just what these *loko* (ponds) did. The *loko 'ume iki* are found only on the islands of Moloka'i and Lāna'i.

*Loko kuapā* means "walled pond," and these were often built of coral or basalt rock in shallow waters protected by reefs. Construction required a great deal of labor to pass large stones hand to hand over several miles. The walled enclosure often utilized a bay or cove and was loosely constructed, allowing water seepage to prevent stagnation within the pond. However, some *loko kuapā* have compact dirt-filled walls. *Mākāhā* connected the pond directly with the ocean. Many of the fishponds on O'ahu are *loko kuapā.*

Some of the Big Island fishponds, such as Lālākea, are of the *loko pu'uone* type, which means they are separated from the sea by a "dune" or "mound of sand." These brackish ponds were connected to the ocean by lanes or streams, and *mākāhā* regulated water circulation and aided in harvesting the fish. The *loko pu'uone* were stream or spring fed, or both, and the water level fluctuated with the rising and falling of the tides.

*Loko wai* were "freshwater ponds," created by diverting a stream into a natural depression. These fishponds were generally small in size; through a buildup of nutrients and freshwater algae, they would turn green or brown in color. The *loko wai* was only indirectly connected to the sea by a channel that let it run off, thereby preventing it from becoming stagnant.

Another inland pond was the *loko i'a kalo. I'a* means "fish," and *kalo* means "taro." *Loko i'a kalo* were "taro fishponds," taro pond fields stocked with fish. Taro, a plant with broad leaves and starchy rootstock, was a main staple of the Hawaiians. It was planted in flooded freshwater pond fields or channels, where *āholehole, 'anae, awa, 'o'opu* (gobies), and *'ōpae'oeha'a* (clawed shrimp) fed upon the ripened stalks. The *loko i'a kalo* demonstrates a sophisticated system of integrated aquaculture and agriculture developed by the ancient Hawaiians.

Most fishponds belonged to the *ali'i*, though some smaller ponds were used by commoners. A *konohiki* oversaw the ponds belonging to royalty and called upon the people for any maintenance required. Everyone partook in the upkeep of fishponds until the *kapu* system was overthrown in 1819 and the *ali'i* gradually lost their power. As foreign diseases were introduced and the native Hawaiian population dwindled, knowledge and expertise in the construction and management of fishponds were lost.

There are some 488 fishponds, large and small, in varying states of disrepair throughout the Hawaiian Islands. If you keep a sharp eye out as you explore coastal areas, you will likely spot the remnants of old fishponds, signs of a unique ancient industry and Hawaiian site.(22; 25; 39; 45; 48)

> "Fishponds were things that beautified the land, and a land with many fishponds was called 'fat.' "
> —S.M. Kamakau (20)

## Fishpond Sites by Region

I     Waiākea Fishpond
         Loko Waka Fishpond

III     Punalu'u Fishpond

IV     Heleipālala Fishpond (Pu'uhonua o Hōnaunau)
         Ka'ūpūlehu Fishpond

V     Ku'uali'i Fishpond ('Anaeho'omalu)
         Kahapapa Fishpond ('Anaeho'omalu)
         Kalāhuipua'a Fishpond and others.

VI     Waipi'o Valley

The sluice gate of the ancient Hawaiian fishpond is called a *mākāhā*. It lets sea water as well as small fish into the pond, but once fish grow fat from feeding inside the pond they can't get out through the narrow openings. The fishpond at Kalāhuipua'a, Kohala, has a fine example of a restored *mākāhā*.

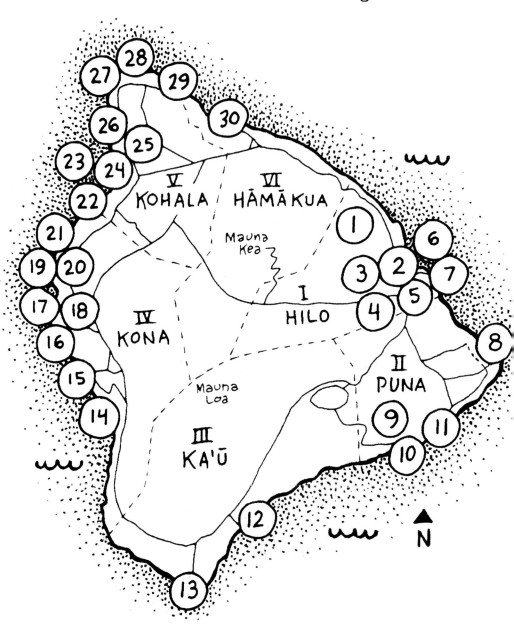

**HAWAI'I
The Big Island**

# SITE LIST BY REGION

Waiākea Fishpond in Hilo.

# SITE LOCATIONS

## I. Hilo

The region of Hilo on the windward side of Hawaiʻi Island may have been named after the first night of the new moon or for a Polynesian navigator. There is also a legend concerning the special twisting (*hilo*) of ti *(kī)* leaves to make a rope for tying up a canoe that crossed the nearby Wailuku River. In any case, the origin of the name Hilo remains uncertain.

Though few archaeological excavations have been carried out in this area, Hilo is known to have supported ancient settlements. Though *heiau* certainly existed in this area, the closest reminders of an ancient temple in the Hilo district are the Naha and the Pinao Pōhaku, sacred stones from the Pinao Heiau. In addition to Pinao Heiau, some of the other temples in this area, now destroyed, were Kaipalaoa, Kānoa, Kīnailoa, and ʻŌhele Heiau. In Laupāhoehoe, North Hilo, were Kamaʻo, Papaulekiʻi, Lonopūlā, Moeapuhi, and Māmala Heiau, all now destroyed.

With two major rivers, numerous streams, and the Waiākea Fishpond, the neighborhood of Hilo Bay is well endowed with water sources, including an annual rainfall of close to 140 inches each year. Numerous dramatic and picturesque waterfalls result from this play of water upon the windward slopes of Mauna Kea and Mauna Loa volcanoes, the highest mountains in the state. The Hawaiian word for waterfall is *wailele*, meaning "leaping water." Noted here are two of the most legendary waterfalls in the Hilo district, ʻAkaka Falls and Waiānuenue or Rainbow Falls.

Other natural features in this area are Ka Waʻa o Māui, Moʻo Kuna, and the Boiling Pots, all on the Wailuku River.

The Lyman House Memorial Museum, 276 Haili Street, in Hilo, has a small exhibition of ancient artifacts in addition to its historical displays and mineral collection. There is an admission fee and tours are available. (See Appendix B, pg. 156) It is well worth a visit before going off in search of ancient sites.

*Hilo 'āina ua lokuloku.*
Hilo of the pouring rain.
—Hawaiian saying (35/107)

## Hilo Region Sites

1. 'Akaka Falls
2. Ka Wa'a o Māui (Māui's Canoe)
3. Waiānuenue (Rainbow Falls)
4. Naha and Pinao Pōhaku
5. Waiākea Fishpond
6. Mokuola (Coconut Island)
7. Loko Waka Fishpond

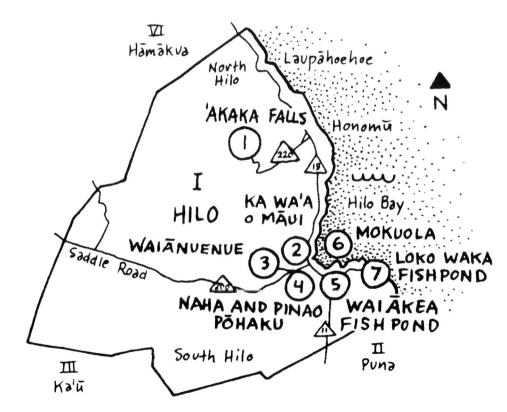

## I.1 'Akaka Falls
*Waterfalls and natural features*

In the midst of the rolling upcountry canefields of Hilo district is the sudden appearance of a gorge filled with dense tropical growth and several splendid waterfalls. *'Akaka* means "a split, chink, or crack," and this is the name of the larger waterfall. Pouring 422 feet into the gorge below, 'Akaka Falls visibly divides the land with its elemental force and natural beauty.

In midstream, seventy feet above the falls, is Pōhaku o Kāloa, a large stone possibly named for the twenty-fourth, twenty-fifth, and twenty-sixth nights of the month. These nights were, according to tradition, sacred to the god Kanaloa.

Another stone in Kolekole Stream at 'Akaka Falls is called Pōhaku o Pele. When this rock is struck with a branch from a *lehua 'apane* tree, it is said that the sky will darken and rain will fall.

Downstream from 'Akaka Falls is the one-hundred-foot-high Kahuna Falls, which can be seen by following the paved and marked .4-mile trail surrounded by bamboo, ferns, and other dense tropical flora. Two other waterfalls, fifteen- and eighteen-feet high, can be seen from the often wet and slippery trail. (14/44, 94; 37/8; 44/65)

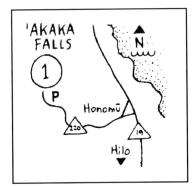

I.1~LOCATION: At the end of Route 220, three miles *ma uka* (towards the mountains) of Honomū, north of Hilo.

## I.2 Ka Wa'a O Māui (Māui's Canoe)
*Natural rock formation*

The rock formation Ka Wa'a O Māui, or "canoe of Māui," was also called Wa'a Kāuhi. It is a distinctive gouge in the river rock of the Wailuku River shaped like a long dugout canoe. The demigod Māui is said to have left it here when in haste he answered the desperate call of his mother, Hina, who was being threatened by a giant *mo'o* (lizard-like creature). Māui had been on the island that now bears his name when Hina called to him for help, and with two strokes of his paddle he quickly bore his magic canoe to the Big Island. He rescued his mother at Waiānuenue (Rainbow Falls), leaving his canoe downriver, and so it remains to this day.

It is said that later Pā'ao, the South Pacific *kahuna*, built a hut on the rock and planted *pili* grass. He was warned by Hina that the rising river waters would destroy his home but he insisted they would not. He was evidently right because, since that time, no matter how swollen the waters of the Wailuku River become, they always remain below the pili grass that sometimes grows by Māui's canoe.

Ka Wa'a O Māui is best viewed from the Pu'ueo Street Bridge or the (Keawe) Wainaku Street bridge in Hilo.

The "canoe" is visible on the south bank of the Wailuku (destructive waters) River. (37/97; 38/26-31).

> *Ka wai lumaluma'i kanaka o Wailuku.*
> The water of Wailuku where men were drowned.
>
> *(Refers to Wailuku, Hilo, where victims were drowned to be offered in sacrifice at a nearby heiau.)*

—Hawaiian saying ( 35/179)

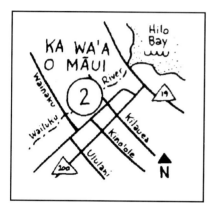

I.2~LOCATION: Between Pu'ueo and Wainaku Streets in the Wailuku River, in the town of Hilo.

## I.3 Waiānuenue (Rainbow Falls)
*Waterfall*

Waiānuenue is the old name for Rainbow Falls and literally means "rainbow [seen in] water." The cave beneath this double falls is the mythic home of the goddess Hina. It is here that Mo'o Kuna, a giant eel-lizard, forced his affections upon the goddess and, when rejected, tried to drown her. As she was about to go under the water for the last time, Hina magically called to her son Māui by sending up the misty cloud, Ao 'ōpua, above the falls. Māui paddled his canoe in two great strokes to bring him from Maui to Hawai'i, left his canoe downriver (Site I.2, pg. 49), and rushed to save his mother by fighting the great *mo'o* in a fierce battle. One of the natural features left as a reminder of this legendary battle is the Boiling Pots. Here the goddess Pelc, at Māui's request, threw hot lava rocks into the river to flush out Mo'o Kuna. The river seems to boil to this day. Finally, Māui slew the monster, whose body now lies below and adjacent to Rainbow Falls in the form of the long black-rock island called Mo'o Kuna.

Wailuku means "destructive waters," a fitting picture for

Wailuku River State Park as it encompasses the Boiling Pots and Waiānuenue. Other waterfalls along the river are Kaimukanaka Falls and Pe'epe'e Falls. (14/94; 37/209; 38/40-45; 44/63)

> *Ka ua lei mā'ohu o Waiānuenue.*
> The rain of Waiānuenue that is like a wreath of mist.
>
> *(Waiānuenue in Hilo, Hawai'i, is now known as Rainbow Falls. On sunny days a rainbow can be seen in the falls, and on rainy days the rising vapor is suggestive of a wreath of mist.)*
> —Hawaiian saying (35/170)

I.3~LOCATION: From Route 200, take Waiānuenue Avenue *ma uka* (toward the mountains) and then turn right, following signs to Rainbow Falls in Wailuku River State Park. Continue 1.4 miles further up Waiānuenue Avenue, turning right on Pe'epe'e Falls Street for the Boiling Pots.

## I.4 Naha and Pinao Pōhaku
*Two large stones*

These two *pōhaku* were a part of the Pinao Heiau, which was situated in the immediate vicinity of Wailuku Drive and Keawe Street, Hilo, on the site of Kūlana Naʻauao. They had been moved to various locations before finding a home in front of the Hilo Public Library.

According to legend, Pōhaku Naha was brought to the Big Island in a double-hulled canoe from Kauaʻi. It weighs an estimated 3.5 tons and served to test claims of royal blood in the *aliʻi* family of Naha. Only a member of the royal family possessed the *mana* (spiritual power) to move the stone. An infant placed upon the venerable stone would remain silent if he were of Naha lineage but would cry if he were not.

More than two centuries ago, the high priestess Kalaniwahine told the young Kamehameha I that he had to fulfill the "overthrowing of a mountain" before his prophesied conquest of the Hawaiian Islands could be accomplished. She advised him as to what he must do, and he departed for Hilo. There, before the high chiefs, the *kahuna* Kalaniwahine, and the assembled people, Kamehameha moved the Naha Pōhaku, even though he was not of the Naha bloodline. Kamehameha later united the Hawaiian Islands into one kingdom under his own rule.

The Pinao Pōhaku is traditionally understood to be a part of the entrance pillar of the Pinao Heiau. Pinao means "dragonfly." (32/34; 37/185; 43/154; 47)

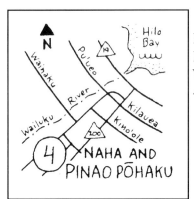

I.4~LOCATION: On the grounds of the Hilo County Public Library, 300 Waiānuenue Street, in Hilo. (Tel: 933-4650).

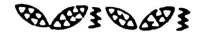

## I.5 Waiākea Fishpond
*Coastal ponds*

Fed by high-volume springs and the Waiākea Stream, then turning into the Wailoa River before emptying into Hilo Bay, Waiākea Fishpond is a natural inland pond located in the town of Hilo. It is actually made up of five ponds: Hōʻakimau, Mohouli, Kalepolepo, Waihole, and the largest, Waiākea, which means "broad waters." Waiākea, which is also spring fed, was once known as the Royal Ponds for it served three generations of the Kamehameha family. Fishing for ʻamaʻama (grey mullet) in former times was *kapu* because that fish was reserved for the king. Today, fishing for ʻamaʻama, *ulua* (jack), and *āholehole* (silver perch) is allowed at Waiākea, which in the past was stocked with *awa* (milkfish) as well. Wailoa, the name of the river into which Waiākea Fishpond flows, literally means "long water," but it is actually the shortest river in the state.

Legend tells of a man named ʻUlu (breadfruit), who, during a time of famine, died of starvation at Waiakea. He was buried near a freshwater spring and the next morning a fully laden breadfruit tree appeared, ending the famine.

The Waiākea area was greatly damaged by the 1946 and 1960 tidal waves. Most of the coastal region is now state and county parks. The Waiākea Fishpond can be approached from various sides and is easily accessible from the bayfront. (25/11-15, 40/93, 37/219)

I.5~LOCATION: In Wailoa State Recreational Area in Hilo. Turn *ma uka* off Kamehameha Avenue, onto Pauahi Street, then take the first left to Visitor Center parking.

## I.6 Mokuola (Coconut Island)
*Small Island*

Mokuola is the old Hawaiian name for the little island in Hilo Bay just offshore from Liliʻuokalani Gardens. Generally known as Coconut Island, Mokuola means "island of life, healing," and it is for this reason that people visited it in ancient times. Not only was the site supposed to have curative spring waters, but those who were able to swim around one of the rocks at an eastern inlet were said to receive special healing.

Tradition speaks of a *puʻuhonua* (place of refuge) on the island, and the umbilical cords of newborn infants were placed here under a flat stone called Papa a Hina. *Mana* (spiritual power) assuring a strong and healthy life beneficial to the child would accrue while the goddess Hina protected the umbilical cord from rats.

There is also a legend that describes Mokuola as a small piece of Maui Island that was broken off when the demigod Māui tried to unite the Valley Isle with Hawaiʻi. Yet another story speaks of Mokuola as the son of ʻUlu (*See* Site I.5, pg. 55).

On the island, to the right of the old landing, is a small sea pool called Puaʻakāheka. This was a special healing spot. Today a bridge allows easy access to Mokuola. (25/15, 37/156)

*Hanu'u ke kai i Mokuola.*
The sea recedes at Mokuola.

*(Now is the opportune time to venture forth. Mokuola, now known as Coconut Island, is a small island in Hilo Bay believed to have curative influences. The sick who swam around it recovered, and a person who could swim around it three times under water would have a long life. When the sea receded, one could swim part way around with little effort.)*
—Hawaiian saying  (34/57)

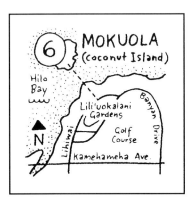

I.6~LOCATION: In Lili'uokalani Gardens, Hilo. Parking is available near the intersection of Banyan Drive and Lihiwai. The island is only accessible by way of a pedestrian footbridge.

## I.7 Loko Waka Fishpond
*Coastal pond*

Loko Waka, also called Loko Aka, is a pond in Keaukaha, Hilo, named for the female *mo'o* (lizard) who dove into the *loko* (pond) in order to escape the jealous anger of Pele, the volcano goddess. Waka, the lizard lady, was unfortunately interested in a man whom Pele also desired. Waka has since been the guardian of the thirty-acre fishpond that is now home to *āholehole*, *'ama'ama*, catfish, trout, and tilapia.

Loko Waka has an enormous water-exchange rate of about 100,000,000 gallons per day, occurring by way of leakage through the surrounding porous lava rock. The commercially successful pond has been used for marine research by the Oceanic Institute and an ornamental pond area features rare white and gold mullet.

The Nakagawa family has leased the state-owned pond for two generations and lately has utilized cage and pen culture in order to increase and better control the fish harvesting. The Nakagawas operate a small restaurant out of their home, adjacent to the pond, serving dinners Tuesday through Sunday. The Seaside Restaurant has become a local favorite, winning national recognition for its fresh steamed fish. (37/134; 48/149-150)

I.7~LOCATION: The Seaside, 1814 Kalaniana'ole Street (Route 137), Hilo (Tel: 935-8835). Two-and-a-half miles east of the intersection of Kamehameha Avenue (19) and Kanoelehua (11).

Pu'u Loa Petroglyph site in Hawai'i Volcanoes National Park, in Puna.

## II  Puna

The Puna district of Hawai'i is situated in the southeastern corner of the island where some of the greatest volcanic activity in Hawai'i takes place.  It is  the youngest region of the entire Hawaiian archipelago.  Its soil is rich and fertile, its beaches are few and often of black sand.

In spite of its newness, Puna, meaning "spring," is home to many ancient sites.  Recently, a network of refuge caves was discovered in this area.  Because of its location on private lands and the archaeological sensitivity of the site, this network and many of the descriptively named sites in Puna are not accessible. To mention just a few, there are the ruins of Mahina Akaaka (clear moon) Heiau near Laeokahuna (point of the secret place), Niukūkahi (coconut standing alone) Heiau, Kohelele O Pele (Pele's Vagina), and Kūki'i (standing image) Heiau.

Sites destroyed by recent lava flows include Kūmaka'ula Heiau, Kekaloa Heiau, the ancient villages of Poupou, Kauka, and Ka'ili'ili, Queen's Bath, the Cave of Refuge, and an eighteenth century *ala* (stone-paved trail); as well as hundreds of other archaeological features. (The above-mentioned trail and other ancient Hawaiian trails were often strewn with small bits of white coral in order to make the trail visible for night travel).  In November 1992, Kamoamoa Campground and its many ancient sites, including the Moa Heiau, were covered with lava;  in 1993, Lae'apuki was destroyed; and in 1997, Waha'ula Heiau was engulfed by a lava flow. Nevertheless, the descriptions of these sites have been left in the book.

Three of the Puna sites described in this book are in the Hawai'i Volcanoes National Park and are relatively close to one another.  They afford an excellent impression of ancient Hawaiian settlement patterns.  A petroglyph field (Pu'u Loa) connected to the birthing rites, agricultural  and fishing villages (Lae'apuki and Kamoamoa), and a high- order *luakini* temple (Waha'ula Heiau), where human sacrifices were conducted, serve to illustrate how over many centuries the ancient Hawaiian people looked upon the journey of life between birth and death. The National Park Service occasionally offers ranger-guided tours of its ancient sites. Check with the Visitors Center for information.

In addition to the sites mentioned above, another curious feature can be visited within the park. In 1790, following an indecisive battle with Kamehameha the Great's army, Keōua, heir to the Big Island, moved his forces in three waves from the Puna district back to Ka'ū. The third wave of warriors discovered all of the second party lying dead, halfway across the Ka'ū desert, apparently killed by toxic volcanic fumes. Heavy volcanic ash and mud also fell in this area, fixing footprints in the lava ground. Though many sets of footprints are found in this region at different lava layers, indicating different time periods, it is believed that some of the imprints are from this tragic flight of Keōua's army. Footprints can be found after a 1.6-mile hike from the Ka'ū Desert Trail Head, ten miles from the Visitors Center along the Belt Road.

In the easternmost region of the Puna district, the place in Hawai'i that receives the first light of dawn, there is a site sacred to the rising sun. Now known as Kumukahi, this spot is remembered as a place of healing and a place of *mana* (spiritual power). It is a natural starting point for a journey to Puna's ancient sites.

> *Weliweli ino Puna i ke akua wahine.*
> Puna dreads the goddess. Puna dreads Pele.
>
> *(Said of any dreaded person.)*
> —Hawaiian saying  (35/321)

## Puna Region Sites

8. Kumukahi
9. Pu'u Loa Petroglyphs
10. Lae'apuki and Kamoamoa
11. Waha'ula Heiau

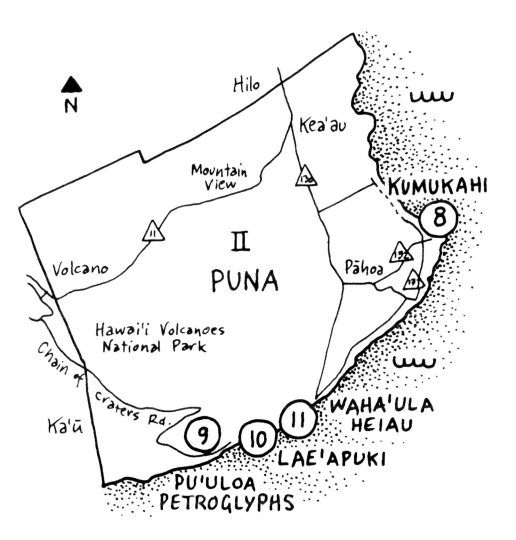

## II.8 Kumukahi

*Coastal area and rock walls*

Cape Kumukahi, "first beginnings," is so named for a migratory hero from Kahiki who landed here and is represented by a large red stone. His two wives, also standing here as large *pōhaku*, were able to manipulate the seasons by pushing the sun back and forth between them. One can only imagine the significance such a tale contains for solar observations that must have taken place at this easternmost point of Hawai'i. It is told that those who worshipped the sun brought their sick to be healed at this place. Kumukahi is also the name of a chief who ridiculed the volcano goddess Pele and thereby received her wrath in the form of the lava flow that created the cape. The cape is also known as King's Pillars. King's Landing, twenty miles further along the coast toward Hilo, is the place where a commoner hit Kamehameha the Great with a paddle while the foot of the *ali'i* was caught in a rock crevice. The king had been chasing innocent fishermen during a battle. Later, he decreed the "Law of the Splintered Paddle," forbidding the accosting of bystanders during both times of war and peace.

A plaque marks the spot. Pāpaʻi (crab) is the old Hawaiian name for King's Landing.

Nearby, atop an old volcanic mound surrounded by a recent lava field, is Kūkiʻi Heiau. The walled platform of common field stone measures more than thirty feet by fifty feet. Kūkiʻi Heiau is presently overgrown with coconut and lauhala trees and only a few rock walls are visible. The floor of the platform around the altar area was at one time covered with flat-hewn lava slabs, all of which have been carried away. Views of the sky and the surrounding area are now blocked by the dense growth of ironwood that covers the hilltop. However, incredible views must once have been possible from this ancient temple, which was traditionally connected to the practice of astronomical observation. It is believed to have been built either by the high chief ʻUmi in the sixteenth century or by Pakaʻa, one generation later. Tradition also says the *heiau* was used for *ʻapu kōheoheo* (poisoning) by *kāhuna*. The *heiau* was still considered significant by King Kalākaua when, in 1877, he brought some of its stones to Honolulu to be used in the construction of the foundation of ʻIolani Palace. (4/8-10; 37/121, 124; 43/151-153; 44/57-58)

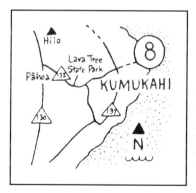

II.8~LOCATION: Take Route 132 east from Pāhoa toward Kapoho and continue straight across Route 137 onto a dirt road. Continue straight to the end of the road where a beacon tower stands. There is no clear footpath across the *aʻā* flow to where a four-wheel-drive track runs along the coast.

## II.9 Pu'u Loa Petroglyphs
*Petroglyph field*

Pu'u Loa means "long hill," and it is here on this desolate stretch of lava that the most concentrated complex of petroglyphs in Hawai'i can be found. The extensive *puka-* or *lua*-glyphs (cup marks and dots) are associated with the practice of leaving the umbilical-cord stump, or *piko*, of a newborn child to collect *mana*, for the health and spiritual strength of the infant. The *piko*, wrapped in *kapa* cloth, was placed in such a carved hole and covered with a stone. Circles (sun signs) are thought to indicate male children (or possibly even calabashes), and semicircles (moon signs) have been suggested to denote female children. Other images such as human figures are also engraved in the *pāhoehoe* (smooth lava) rock at this site.

Though petroglyphs can be found throughout this area of Puna, the most interesting site is beside the so-called "long [life] hill", (Pu'u Loa). A short, .7-mile, hike along a well-worn ancient foot path is required to reach the complex where a viewing platform is provided in order to save the petroglyphs from trampling underfoot and to allow an elevated perspective. (8/21-32; 27/6, 50; 32/25-26, 38; 37/200-201)

Some *ki'i pōhaku* that were saved from a recent lava flow can be viewed in the Visitors Center. These petroglyphs will eventually be returned to their original locations once the lava flow stabilizes.

(Pu'u Loa is also the old name for Queen's Bath, a natural freshwater pool in the Royal Gardens area that was covered by a 1988 lava flow. The pool was a long, narrow, grotto-like trough where Hawaiian royalty were said to have bathed in ancient times. The cool mountain-fed bath was also used and appreciated more recently by local people and tourists aware of its location. Residents of the area warned that Pele was discontented with the trash and irreverent use of the pool and predicted that she would one day reclaim it.)

Remember that viewing and photographing petroglyphs are best done early in the morning or late in the afternoon. Please do not walk on petroglyph images or deface them in any way. Rubbings cause damage.

Hawaiian sailing canoes were often the subject of *ki'i pōhaku* as can be seen in this striking example at Pu'u Loa in Puna.

*Kālele ka uwahi o Pu'uloa.*
The smoke of Pu'uloa leans over.

*(Said in amusement of one who leans over,
intent on his work.)*

—Hawaiian saying  (35/156)

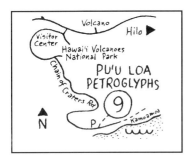

II.9~LOCATION: About seventeen miles down Chain of Craters Road from the Hawai'i Volcanoes National Park Visitors Center. Watch for Park Service signs indicating parking. Hike about .7 miles *ma uka* (towards the mountains) of Chain of Craters Road. Entrance fee.

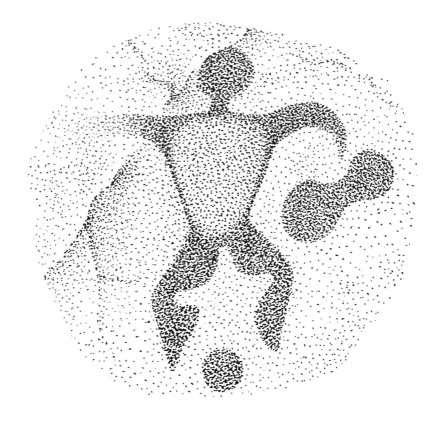

Among the many petroglyph images at Pu'u Loa is the graceful figure of a "dancer with *ipu*" (gourd percussion instrument).

## II.10 ~ Lae'apuki and Kamoamoa
*Rock enclosures, platforms, petroglyphs*
*(all sites now covered with lava)*

The ancient village of Lae'apuki was a residential complex that was abandoned in the early 1920's after it had been converted from a farming and fishing community to a goat- and cattle-herding village. In the early 1990's, the site consisted of numerous low rock walls in a rather overgrown condition, situated beside the coast and just less than a mile from the former Kamoamoa village. Both village sites are now covered with lava.

Kamoamoa village, fronted by a spectacular black-sand beach and shaded by many Hawaiian plants, was an ancient farming and fishing community destroyed in 1868 by a tsunami and later turned into a campground by the Hawai'i Volcanoes National Park. In spite of the destruction, many interesting features remained, including numerous low rock enclosures and walls (the remains of a residential complex), a house site and canoe shed, petroglyphs, several burial mounds, and an agricultural *heiau*. Most of these were covered by lava in November 1992. The temple at Kamoamoa was known as Moa Heiau and was considered to be of the Hale o Lono type, dedicated to the god of agriculture and fertility. This assumption of use was based both on its size (it was not as large as the *luakini* [sacrificial] type), and on its location (just to the west of Kamoamoa was a large enclosed area with hundreds of agricultural features such as sweet potato mounds). The National Park Service was planning to feature the ancient sites at Kamoamoa in a new educational program at the park when an unexpected lava flow consumed the entire area. (28/25-31, 58-66; 34/28-35; 37/82)

Lae'apuki was also reclaimed by lava shortly after the destruction of Kamoamoa; it was the last ancient village site in this area. As this occurred during the writing of this book, it seemed appropriate to leave both sites in the text. Do not, however, expect to see anything here but a barren lava field. Hiking in this area where active flows occur is restricted.

II.10~LOCATION: Ma kai (toward the sea), off the Chain of Craters Road, about twenty-two miles from the Visitors Center in Hawai'i Volcanoes National Park. Entrance fee.

Carved wooden *ki'i* or image with comb crest. One interpretation designates this figure as the volcano goddess, Pele. (15/484)

## II.11 Waha'ula Heiau
*Rock wall enclosures (now covered by lava)*

Waha'ula means "red mouth," and the ancient temple that goes by this name is believed to have been the first *luakini heiau* in all of Hawai'i. It is closely associated with the *kahuna* Pā'ao and human sacrifice, and it may also be linked with the goddess Pele and the local volcanic activity. Its original name may have been 'Aha'ula, which means "royal assembly"; tradition holds that at one time it was served by ten or more *kāhuna*.

The Waha'ula complex consisted of two major structures, both low stonewall enclosures, one about 10,000 square feet, the other over 18,000 square feet. Many other archaeological features, including a *pu'uhonua* (place of refuge), were located here. One of the two larger temple enclosures is believed to have been built by Pā'ao around 1275 A.D. Pā'ao, a *kahuna* from the legendary Kahiki, is credited with introducing a new religio-political system that heightened the distinctions between the *ali'i* class and the commoners. He is also said to have initiated the practice of human sacrifice.

Smoke from the sacred Waha'ula sanctuary carried such a harsh *kapu* that anyone caught passing under its path was

put to death.  A small cave below the jagged *a'ā* coastline south
of the *heiau* was used as a place to clean the bones of human
sacrifices and is called Holoināiwi (bone washer).

It is generally accepted that Waha'ula is a tenth-to-
thirteenth century *heiau*. It has been stated, however, that parts
of the religious complex could have been built as early as the
fifth century, judging from the age of lava flows in this area. (27/
4) The *heiau* was reconditioned by Chief 'Imaikalani of Ka'ū around
1500 A.D., and again by Kalani'ōpu'u around 1770 A.D.
Kamehameha I carried out the final renovations at Waha'ula in
early historic times, dedicating it to Kūkā'ilimoku, god of war.  In
the early nineteenth century, Liholiho (Kamehameha II) made a
point of visiting Waha'ula during the time of the Makahiki (a four-
month festive period of peace begining in the autumn). Waha'ula
Heiau was the last major temple to have worship open to the
public, which is unusual because *luakini heiau* were generally
closed to all but *ali'i* and *kāhuna*.

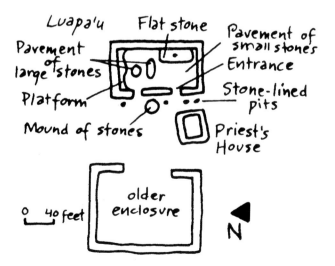

Waha'ula Heiau in Puna is believed to be the first
Hawaiian *luakini* or human sacrifice temple built by
Pā'ao in about the thirteenth century and later rebuilt
by 'Imaikalani in the sixteenth century.  Kalani'ōpu'u
and finally Kamehameha renovated the *heiau* in the
eighteenth century.  Present-day lava flows have
destroyed this ancient site. (Plan based on Stokes.)

In 1989, a lava flow crossed the Chain of Craters Road, destroyed a Hawai'i Volcanoes National Park Visitors Center, covered hundreds of recorded archaeological sites (including Queen's Bath, and Ka'ili'ili, Poupou, and Kauka ancient villages), flowed up to and around both sides of Waha'ula Heiau, and then poured into the sea. Everything for miles around was covered by the heavy black blanket of *pele* (lava)—except for the main walls of the ancient temple. Some lava did enter the older, larger structure but left its walls intact. In August of 1997, just before the second printing of this book, Waha'ula was covered by another lava flow. Nothing of this *heiau* can be seen although its location will surely be long remembered. Hiking in the area is not permitted. Viewing is possible only by helicopter.

A large scale model of the *heiau*, constructed by John Stokes, can be seen at the Bishop Museum in Honolulu. The model is built from stone and wood collected at the Waha'ula site. (14/53-54; 16/137, 160; 26/158; 28/56-58; 31; 37/218; 43/136-144)

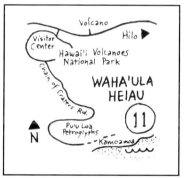

II.11~LOCATION: Within Hawai'i Volcanoes National Park. Entrance fee.

Offering platform at Kalalea Heiau, a temple dedicated to fishing.

# III  Ka'ū

Ka'ū district is the southernmost region of Hawai'i and of the United States.  It includes the summit of Mauna Loa (long mountain), a 13,679-foot active volcano, and stretches down to Ka Lae, known as South Point, at sea level.  The district encompasses the Great Ka'ū Desert and the most active volcano in the world, Kīlauea, which means "spewing and spreading," both in the Hawai'i Volcanoes National Park.

The meaning of the name Ka'ū has long been forgotten.  However, it is an ancient word related to the Samoan Ta'ū.  The old name for Ka'ū was Ka'ūloa, "long Ka'ū."

Ka'ū has thousands of sites from ancient paved trails and lava tube burial caves with petroglyphs to village ruins, fishponds, and *heiau* platforms.  In the windy South Point area many important archaeological features can be observed, such as the ancient canoe moorings, salt pan rocks, and *heiau* sites.  Punalu'u was an important region of Hawaiian settlement with its numerous *heiau*, fishponds, and other natural features.

Some of the temple sites not explored by this book are Lanipao Heiau, at Punalu'u, said to have been built by Laka of Kaua'i; Ke'ekū Heiau, overlooking Kawa'a Bay; 'Imakakaloa Heiau, at Ka'alā'iki, devoted to *hula*; Pa o Kua Heiau, at Kahaea, reputed to have been used for *ho'omanamana* (wizardry) by a local *kahuna*; Malulani Heiau, at Kiolaka'a, which was also a *pu'uhonua* (place of refuge); Mōlīlele Heiau, commanding an extensive view of the South Point region, and Pākini Heiau, a *heiau  ho'oulu 'ai* (temple where first crops were offered) associated with the rebel Puna chief, 'Imakaloa.

> *I puni ia 'oe o Ka'ū a i'ike'ole*
> *'oe ia Ka'ūloa, 'a'ohe no 'oe i*
> *'ike ia Ka'ū.*
> If you have been around Ka'ū
> and have not seen Ka'ūloa,
> you have not seen the whole of the district.

*(Ka'ūloa and Wai'ohinu were two stones, wife and husband, that stood in a kukui grove on the upper side of the road between Na'alehu and Wai'ohinu. With the passing of time, these stones gradually sank until they vanished completely into the earth. After Ka'ūloa was no longer seen, Palahemo* [An inland water hole at South Point, believed to be connected to the sea and inhabited by a *mo'o.* Palahemo means "loose dab of excreta."] *was substituted as the chief point of interest.)*

—Hawaiian saying   (35/136)

## Ka'ū Region Sites

12. Punalu'u
13. Kalalea Heiau

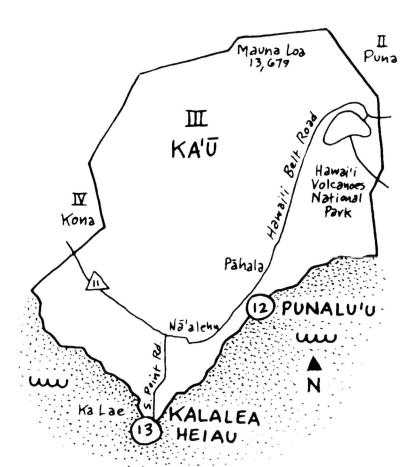

## III.12 Punalu'u

*Fishpond, heiau, petroglyphs*

Enclosed on one side by the grey-black sands of Punalu'u Beach and surrounded by low-growing coconut palms is a "sweet water" pond, no longer producing fish as in the old days but providing a picturesque view for beach-goers and visitors dining at the Punalu'u Restaurant. This is Punalu'u Fishpond. Separated from Kūhua Bay by sixty yards of beach, the brackish water pond is fed by a spring called Kawaihū o Kauila. Kauila is the legendary turtle goddess who protects and cares for the spring and the pond. Punalu'u means the "spring dived for."

The mythological figure Laka is also connected with Punalu'u, for tradition tells how he slew the man-eating *mo'o*, Kaikapū, whose pretty granddaughter would lead unsuspecting travelers into her grandmother's cave where they would be devoured.

Overlooking the Punalu'u Fishpond are the impressive remains of Kāne'ele'ele Heiau, a stone platform measuring not less than seven-hundred feet long by five-hundred feet wide. Its size suggests, as does local tradition, that Kāne'ele'ele was the district *luakini* (human sacrifice) temple. It is said to be two *heiau* set end to end: Halelau in the south and Punalu'u Nui in the north, but it is also known by the name Mailekini Heiau. In 1906 there was still a large, flat "sacrificial stone" outside the southern wall of the *heiau*, and bone pits were discovered during construction of a small warehouse along the west side of the precinct. A restored wooden *lele* or offering stand shows the *heiau* is still visited by twentieth-century worshippers.

Another temple site in this area is Ka'ie'ie Heiau, named for the *'ie'ie* vine. Across from Sea Mountain Golf Clubhouse, its low standing rock walls can be seen from the beach at Nīnole Cove, west of Punalu'u Beach Park. It sits at the edge of an *'a'ā* lava flow above the sea and alongside the old government road. Nīnole Cove was also home to an ancient fishpond, now destroyed.

Adjacent to the Punalu'u Beach restrooms are several faded petroglyph figures carved in smooth coastal rocks. Dozens of other *ki'i pōhaku* were destroyed when the nearby parking lot was constructed. Local school children now monitor and act as guardians of the remaining petroglyphs. (11/212-214; 16/137, 160; 19/40; 23/22-36; 37/105, 165, 194; 43/131-133; 44/49)

*Ka'ili'ili hānau o Kōloa;*
*ka nalu ha'i o Kāwā.*
The reproducing pebbles of Kōloa;
the breaking surf of Kāwā.

*(In Punalu'u, Ka'ū, is a small beach called Kōloa.*
*The pebbles found here were believed to re-*
*produce—the smooth ones being males and the*
*porous ones females. These were considered the*
*best on the island of Hawai'i for* hula 'ili'ili. [Small,
smooth, water-worn stones that are used in *hula*
to make a clicking sound as an accompaniment.]
*Kāwā is just beyond Kōloa toward Honu'apo).*

—Hawaiian saying (35/152)

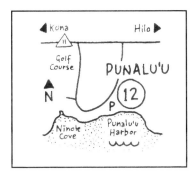

III.12~LOCATION: Off the Hawai'i Belt Road and at the eastern end of Punalu'u (black sand) Beach County Park.

## III.13 Kalalea Heiau
*Stone enclosure, canoe moorings, salt pans*

At Ka Lae, "the point," on the southernmost end of Hawai'i, is a well-preserved fishing shrine known as Kalalea Heiau or Hale o Kalalea. This South Point location is believed to be the first land sighted by Polynesian voyagers sailing for Hawai'i, and it was said to be a place for planning and preparing long-distance voyages to the South Pacific as well as a place for offering thanks for safe arrivals.

Kalalea Heiau, *kapu* to women, is believed to be dedicated to fishing. Offerings are still left at the site today as the South Point waters attract modern-day fisherman just as they did in the past.

The small *heiau* enclosure measures forty-three by thirty-five feet, with two smaller platforms outside the structure adjoining the western wall. On the main platform is a *pōhaku* called Kumaiea (female), but also attributed to Kāne, and on the smaller platform just *ma uka* is another upright stone called Kānemakua (male), associated with the god Kanaloa. Standing twelve feet to the north of the *heiau* are two more stones, the northerly one called 'Ai'ai, the son of Kū'ula. Within the *heiau*, beside the *ma uka* wall, is a rock called Kū'ula, the god of fishermen. Hina, the wife of Ku'ula, is said to live in a sea cave just offshore from Kalalea Heiau.

A rock at the water's edge here is called Pōhakuwa'a Kāuhi, "Kāuhi canoe stone," and is a constant reminder of the canoe journeys made from Kahiki. Another offshore stone at South Point is called Pōhakuokeau, "stone of the current," referring to the meeting of the different ocean currents that come together here. It also means "stone of the times," referring to a belief that the stone would turn over whenever there was a change in the government.

Holes carved into the shoreline lava rock were used as moorings by the ancient Hawaiians. Handcarved salt pans can also be seen in this area. Sea water was trapped in shallow dish-like rocks and then allowed to evaporate leaving the sea salt behind. Along the eastern side of the point excavations have uncovered a site used at least one-thousand years ago as a place for fishhook manufacturing.

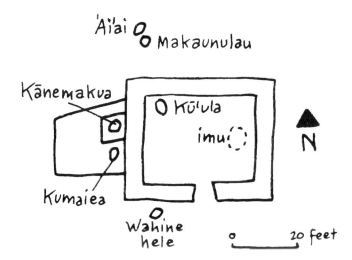

Kalalea Heiau in Ka'ū is a small fisherman's temple said to have been built by *Menehune.* Within the enclosure is Pōhaku Kupua (Kū'ula), a place for offering one's first catch, and an *imu* (oven) for cooking food offerings. (Based on Stokes's plan).

Also nearby are Mākālei Cave and the well, Lua o Palahemo. The well has a petroglyph image on its rim.

Much of Ka Lae is Hawaiian Home Lands, land formerly owned by the Hawaiian monarchy and now held in trust for the Hawaiian people. This area, including the *heiau*, is a National Historic Landmark.

Ka Lae on Hawai'i, like Ka'ena Point on O'ahu, Pu'u Keka'a on Maui, and the northshore *pali* above Kalaupapa on Moloka'i, is considered *leina a ka 'uhane* (leap of the soul), a "jumping-off" place for the souls of the dead on their journey into the next world. It is here that at the end of life the departed soul makes the leap to Pō. (1/94-95; 21; 26/158-59; 36/71, 73-74; 43/115-119; 44/48)

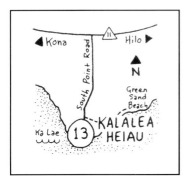

III.13~LOCATION: At the end of South Point Road, ten miles *ma kai* of Hawai'i Belt Road, Highway 11. (Note: Most rental car companies do not allow their vehicles on South Point Road.)

Ka Lae (the point) was a frequented fishing spot and canoe landing site. Visitors can still see ancient canoe mooring holes carved through the shoreline lava rock.

Kalalea Heiau at Ka Lae in Ka'ū, a temple that tradition holds is dedicated to fishing and long distance ocean voyaging.

A master carver in the canoe shed at Pu'uhonua o Hōnaunau National Historical Park.

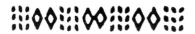

## IV Kona

The Kona district of Hawai'i is one of the richest archaeological regions in the archipelago. It is one of the most studied, surveyed, excavated, and preserved areas in spite of, and in part due to, the development that has occurred here. One seven-mile stretch of the Kona coast contains more than twenty-five *heiau*, and large portions of the region are on the National Register of Historic Places. Acknowledgment must be given to the local government's efforts in requiring adequate archaeological surveys and salvage excavations in connection with on-going development.

Besides the abundance of temple sites, there are also numerous settlement ruins, lava tube caves used for burial, refuge, and habitation, *hōlua* (sled courses), and late prehistoric and early historic battlegrounds.

The interior of Keikipu'ipu'i Heiau, or the King's temple (referring to Kamehameha II, Liholiho), shows large wooden *ki'i* of the gods, wooden *lele* (altar) offering platform (with remains of an animal sacrifice), and *anu'u* tower draped with leaves. This *luakini heiau* was probably built around the time of the high chief 'Umi, and was restored in the time of Kalani'opu'u. It stood on the south shore of Kailua Bay. No trace of it remains today. (After J. Arago, early ninteenth century.)

Most of the ancient sites in Kona are not isolated from each other but related to nearby sites. From the National Parks of Pu'uhonua o Hōnaunau in South Kona to Kaloko-Honokōhau in North Kona, most of the sites are complexes as opposed to single features.

Though only coastal sites are dealt with here, extensive upland field systems associated with residential compounds can be found in the Kona district. Ahua 'Umi Heiau, used by the sixteenth century paramount chief 'Umi, is an upcountry temple site that served North Kona.

The North Kona area between Keauhou and Kailua was a major population center in the late prehistoric period and an important seat of political power well into early historic times. Both written and oral histories make this clear and are supported by the archaeological finds in this area.

Some of the fishponds found in ancient Kona were Pa'aiea, Kualana, 'Ōpae'ula, Kūki'o, Waiakuhi, Ka'ūpūlehu, Kīholo, Luahinewai, Wainānāli'i, Keawaiki, and Weliweli.

*O na hōkū o ka lani luna,*
*o Pa'aiea ko lalo.*
The stars are above, Pa'aiea below.

*(Refers to Kamehameha's great fishpond, Pa'aiea, in Kona, Hawai'i. Its great size led to this say-ing; the small islets that dotted its interior were compared to the stars that dot the sky. The pond was destroyed during a volcanic eruption in 1801.)*
　　　　　　　　　　　　　　—Hawaiian saying  (35/275)

The conservation of Kona's ancient sites is managed by many different groups. Pu'uhonua o Hōnaunau and Kaloko Honokōhau are in the care of the National Parks Service. Hikiau Heiau is protected by the State of Hawai'i, and Ahu'ena Heiau and the entire Keauhou complex are managed by private hotels. The native Hawaiian community and numerous civic groups also pour enormous amounts of time and energy into the care and protection of their ancient sites.

The Kuakini Room of Hulihe'e Palace in Kailua-Kona, 75-5718 Ali'i Drive, open 9 A.M. to 4 P.M. daily, has a fine collection of late prehistoric artifacts and early historic antiques. Supervised by The Daughters of Hawai'i, the palace offers guided tours and charges an admission fee (Tel: 329-1877).

In Captain Cook, on the main road, Highway 11, is the Kona Historic Society Museum. It has a small collection of mostly historic artifacts. One should call to check on visiting hours (Tel: 323-3222).

The Kona Outdoor Circle has begun restoration of a complex of three *heiau* known collectively as Heiau Kealakōwa'a. The ancient temple site is located on Outdoor Circle property just off Kuakini Highway near the Lako Street exit. Kealakōwa'a was used for blessing canoes made of *koa* logs, which were harvested on Mt. Hualālai. The high priest presented offerings at a second temple within the enclosure. The third temple, Kilolani, was an astronomical *heiau*, used by chief councils and *kāhuna*. An encircling wall is being restored and visitors will be able to view demonstrations of Hawaiian canoemaking in a replica canoe shed. A trail with interpretive signs will also be established. At the time of this writing, clearing of the platforms has begun but interpretive displays are not yet complete. The site is nevertheless open to the public. Call Kona Outdoor Circle for further information (Tel: 808-329-7286).

The Amy Greenwell Ethnobotanical Garden in the town of Captain Cook is an ethnobotanical research station that maintains an ancient Kona agricultural field system. Operated by the Bishop Museum, it is open to the public and offers guided tours. Call 808-323-3318 for information.

*Māmā Kona i ka wai kau mai i ka maka o ka 'ōpua.*
Kona is lightened in having water in the face of the clouds.

*(Kona is relieved, knowing that there will be no drought, when the clouds promise rain).*

—Hawaiian saying  (35/232)

## Kona Region Sites

14. Pu'uhonua o Hōnaunau
15. Hikiau Heiau
16. Kamehameha III Birthplace
17. Keauhou
18. Ku'emanu Heiau
19. Ahu'ena Heiau
20. Kaloko-Honokōhau
21. Ka'ūpūlehu

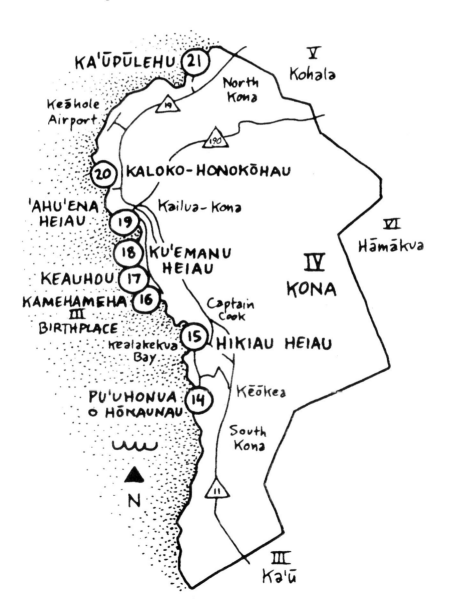

## IV.14 Puʻuhonua o Hōnaunau
National Historical Park
*Stone platforms and walls, restored wooden images and thatched structures, fishpond, canoe landing, petroglyph, and cave.*

In ancient times, Puʻuhonua o Hōnaunau was a safe haven to *kapu* (taboo) breakers, defeated warriors, deserters, and refugees of all kinds. (Punishment for breaking many *kapu* was death.) If a *kapu* breaker made his way to the *puʻuhonua* without being captured, he could be pardoned of his crime after a series of ritual procedures administered by the local *kāhuna*.

Several places of refuge were located on each of the Hawaiian Islands and they helped to balance the rather severe scale of *kapu* justice. Puʻuhonua o Hōnaunau was not desecrated in 1819 when the traditional religious practices were abolished and temples were destroyed because the Kamehameha dynasty was connected to this place. Many of their ancestors' bones were kept here and, therefore, the site was revered and protected.

The *pu'uhonua* is dated at about 1550 A.D. by the National Park Service and is partially enclosed by a ten-foot-high, seven-foot-thick, one-thousand-foot-long, uniquely constructed lava rock wall separating the refuge from an *ali'i* residence. No mortar holds this massive rock wall together. On the royal grounds are Heleipōlala Fishpond and the royal canoe landing at Keone'ele Cove, both once forbidden to commoners. As this area was *kapu*, refuge seekers had to swim across Hōnaunau Bay in order to reach the *pu'uhonua*. Within the enclosure are three *heiau* platforms of varying dates. The most recent of these, Hale o Keawe, from about 1650 A.D., has been restored with a thatched *hale* (house), *ki'i* (images) carved from *'ōhi'a* logs, a wooden *lele* (altar) for offerings, and a wooden fence. This building served as the temple mausoleum, housing the bones of some twenty-three chiefs, beginning with Keaweikehahiali'iokamoku. The *mana* (spiritual power) of these bones gave greater power and protection to the *pu'uhonua*. Hale o Keawe was first known as Ka Iki 'Āle'ale'a, the "little light of joy."

Once within the refuge precinct, a *kapu* breaker would be absolved by a *kahuna pule* (priest). Sometimes the offender would be free to return home within only a few hours, other times days were required for purification ceremonies. In 1782, a battle at Moku'ōhai three miles to the north drove many defeated warriors to seek refuge at Pu'uhonua o Hōnaunau. There was one recourse for those who could not reach a refuge: A high chief or chiefess could act as a *pu'uhonua* and forgive *kapu* breakers of their crimes. Queen Ka'ahumanu was such a *pu'uhonua*.

Also within the refuge precinct is the older 'Āle'ale'a Heiau, a striking raised platform used by chiefs for sports and games after Hale o Keawe was constructed. Beside the *heiau* is Keōua Stone, a legendary resting place of the high chief Keōua. Six post-holes may have supported columns for a canopy above this spot. On the other side of 'Āle'ale'a platform is the Ka'ahumanu Stone, where the favorite wife of Kamehameha I hid after a lovers' quarrel. Her absolution apparently worked for she remained the favorite of the first monarch.

Closer to the ocean is yet another, older, *heiau* that remains unexcavated, its name lost to history.

A single petroglyph of a human figure can also be seen within the *pu'uhonua*. The technique and full-outline style indicate it may be of the late prehistoric or early historic period.

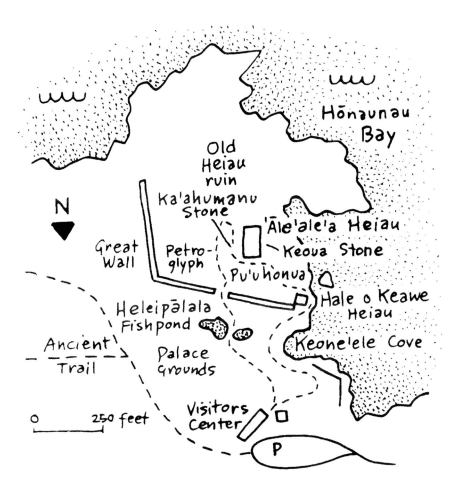

When the *kapu* system was abandoned by Kamehameha II and *heiau* were ordered destroyed, Hale o Keawe was likely spared because of its sacred history as a mausoleum for the Kamehameha lineage. However, Queen Ka'ahumanu ordered the ancestral bones removed and the temple dismantled in 1829.

In 1920, this area, then called the City of Refuge, became a county park after sitting in ruin for almost one hundred years. In 1961, the 180 acres were donated to the federal government by Bishop Estate (the trust handling the estate of Princess Bernice Pauahi Bishop, who died in 1884), and, in 1978, it became a National Historical Park under the name of Pu'uhonua o Hōnaunau.

Just beyond the park Visitors Center is an 1871 trail that leads to Ki'ilae Village ruins and a number of other archaeological features including 'Ōma'o Heiau, Alahaka Heiau, Kēōkea Hōlua, and Waiūohina lava tube. The village is not considered very ancient, dating back only to the late 1700s. It lies .75 miles south of Pu'uhonua o Hōnaunau. Further details on this and other sites in the area can be obtained from the National Park Service Visitors Center.

Hale o Keawe Heiau at Pu'uhonua o Hōnaunau (Site IV.14 pg. 89), served as the repository for the bones of twenty-three chiefs of Hawai'i, beginning with Keawe. The site has been restored to look much like it did when the first Western explorers glimpsed it during the early historic period. (Based on a drawing by Rev. William Ellis, 1822-23.)

Regular orientation talks, cultural events, and other activities are sponsored by the National Park Service and a brochure with a self-guided tour is available. (1/94-95; 5; 9/313; 11/163-171; 14/50-52; 16/137-139; 26/161-165; 34/95-219; 37/10,38, 196; 42; 43/104-107; 44/46)

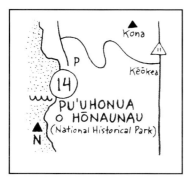

IV.14~LOCATION: Off Route 160 on the south shore of Hōnaunau Bay. Pu'uhonua o Hōnaunau National Historic Park, Hōnaunau, Kona, Hawai'i, 96726. (Tel: 328-2288) Entrance fee.

The Great Wall that divides the place of refuge from the *ali'i* residence at Pu'uhonua o Hōnaunau.

## IV.15 Hikiau Heiau
*Raised stone platform*

    Hikiau means "moving current" and the *heiau* is located beside a famous ancient surfing beach. Directly on the edge of the sand, the magnificent *heiau* platform is of the *luakini* (human sacrifice) type and is known to have been used by Kamehameha I.

    The *heiau* platform, built on the edge of an *a'ā* lava flow, is 16-feet high at its northwestern corner and was originally more than 250-feet long and over 100-feet wide. A smaller platform is built up three feet from the larger foundation and presumably carried the *lele* (altar).

    This state monument at Kealakekua (pathway [of] the god) Bay is also where the British naval captain, James Cook, was welcomed by Hawaiians as Lono, the god of agriculture and prosperity. Cook's ship arrived during the months of the Makahiki, a festival honoring Lono with tribute offerings, feasting, competitive games, and *hula* performances, lasting from November through February. All warring was suspended during this time. The god's ensignia was an upright pole with crossbeam and hanging tapa cloth, not so unlike the mast and sails of a European ship. Captain Cook was accorded all the hospitality due a divine guest. Besides attending a Hawaiian ceremony at a Kealakekua *heiau* given in his honor, Captain Cook performed the first Christian ceremony in Hawai'i at Hikiau Heiau, a funeral service for a crew member, William Whatman, who died January 28, 1779. However, when the British visitors left and then were suddenly forced to return to repair a broken mast, the Makahiki had ended and attitudes had changed. It was at this time that Captain Cook was killed in a skirmish over Chief Kalani'ōpu'u, whom Cook had tried to take as a hostage in return for a small boat that had been stolen from his ship and later broken up by Hawaiians for its iron nails. A white obelisk on the north side of the bay and an underwater plaque now mark the spot where the explorer lost his life. Cook's body was taken to Puhina o Lono Heiau, which means "burning of Lono," for traditional Hawaiian rites that included burning and cleaning flesh from the bones.

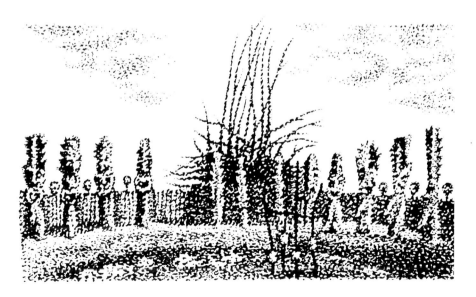

Hikiau Heiau, built by Kalani'ōpu'u at Kealakekua Bay, was visited by Captain James Cook in 1778-79. This drawing is based on a sketch by Cook's surgeon, William Ellis, in which he noted numerous *akua ki'i* (wooden images of the gods) and a *lele* (offering stand) with gourd rat guards, within the sacred compound.

To the north, near Hikiau, was a sacred pond and a small village. The black sand beach here has not yet returned since Hurricane 'Iniki struck the islands in 1992.

Some forty other temples, most of them on private property, are in this area around the bay and above Ka'awaloa. Moku'ōhai Battleground (1782) is not far to the south.

Hikiau Heiau is a registered state monument. (9/290-291, 296; 16/115, 160; 26/164-166; 37/45, 101; 43/98-102 )

IV.15~LOCATION: Outside of Captain Cook off Highway 11, in Kealakekua Bay State Historical Park, Nāpo'opo'o, South Kona.

# IV.16 Kamehameha III Birthplace
*Large stones*

Here beside Keauhou Bay is the birth site of Kalani Kauikeaouli. He was born on August 11, 1813, the son of Kamehameha I and Keōpūolani, the king's highest-ranking wife. Following the deaths of Kamehameha I in Kailua-Kona and Kamehameha II (his older brother, Liholiho) in England, Kalani Kauikeaouli was declared King Kamehameha III on June 6, 1825, by a council of ruling chiefs.

Since the new king was only eleven years old at the time, Ka'ahumanu, the favorite wife of Kamehameha the Great, was installed as first *kuhina nui* or "prime minister," along with *ali'i* Kalanimoku as a special guardian. (The office of *kuhina nui* was abolished in 1864.)

Kamehameha III grew up in the Keauhou region and was very rebellious as a youth. He defied the Christian teachings that Ka'ahumanu and the ruling chiefs embraced, and he urged a return to the old ways of premissionary times. He spent much of his time drinking, surfing, and gambling until the death of his beloved twenty-year-old sister in 1836. With this sad event, the young king completely changed his ways, giving up drinking and mending his lifestyle. A year later, Kamehameha III married Kalama, daughter of a minor Kona *ali'i*, and turned his attention toward the ruling of his small Pacific nation.

During his reign France seized the Marquesas, 2400 miles to the south of Hawai'i, and established a protectorate in Tahiti. In Hawai'i, a Declaration of Rights as well as a Constitution was written. Great Britain annexed New Zealand and unexpectedly took possession of Hawai'i for a few brief months in 1843. When Hawaiian independence was restored by a proclamation from Queen Victoria, the Hawaiian king is said to have declared: *"Ua mau ke ea o ka 'āina i ka pono"* (The sovereignty of the land is perpetuated in righteousness), which has since become the state motto.

Before his death on December 15, 1854, Kamehameha III had been discussing with the United States the possibility of Hawaiian annexation. But Alexander Liholiho, his adopted son and heir to the throne, broke off negotiations as his first official act as King Kamehameha IV.

First protected by The Daughters of Hawai'i, the birth site is a natural arrangement of stones surrounded by a rock wall, indicating where the sacred life of this *ali'i*, Kamehameha III, began.

Above the birthplace, *ma uka* (towards the mountains) of Ali'i Drive, is the Keauhou Hōlua Slide National Historic Landmark. The *hōlua* is a stone-paved incline used by the *ali'i* to test their courage and skills in sled racing. The sled course was covered with mats and grasses to make it slick for the wooden runners of a narrow sled. The Keauhou sled course originally went all the way down to the sea. It is the longest and best preserved *hōlua* in Hawai'i. This site is unmarked, overgrown, and in disrepair. A model of a *hōlua* sled can be seen at the Hulihe'e Palace in Kailua-Kona. (19/429-446; 37/104; 44/43-44)

Also close by Kamehameha III Birthplace is the Kuamo'o Battle Burial Ground, where the *ali'i* and *kahuna*, Kekuaokalani, died in 1819 as he unsuccessfully led the forces opposing the abolition of the *kapu* system and the destruction of *heiau* and sacred images. With this defeat, ancient Hawaiian religious practices were driven into hiding by the ruling Hawaiian government.

IV.16~LOCATION: Beside Keauhou Bay, at the end of Keleopapa Road, off Ali'i Drive. Marked by a Hawai'i Visitors Bureau sign.

*Kepie* is the old Hawaiian name for the eight-to-ten-foot-long wooden sled used in *hōlua*, a sled course sport. A scale replica of the *kepie*, which was raced by the *ali'i* down specially constructed stone inclines, can be seen at the Hulihe'e Palace, in Kailua-Kona. (18/60)

## IV.17 Keauhou
*Numerous rock wall enclosures and platforms, upright stones, petroglyphs, ponds, and canoe landing*

The grounds of Keauhou Beach Hotel and several miles of the Kona coast in this area are on the National Register of Historic Places. The Keauhou complex is clearly sacred land with its three *heiau*, the King's Pond, *kū'ula* stones, petroglyphs, freshwater springs, and rich mythic traditions blending with factual history.

The petroglyphs at Keauhou lie just offshore at the southwest end of the complex, usually underwater but nonetheless visible. (At one time, the land was higher but earthquakes in the past few hundred years have shifted the shoreline.) One of the twenty-four petroglyphs is said to be the likeness of Chief Kamalālāwalu, a Maui Island *ali'i* sacrificed at Ke'ekū Heiau.

Ke'ekū Heiau, built by Lonoikamakahiki, was a *luakini heiau* that also served as a *pu'uhonua*. Kamalālāwalu of Maui was beheaded and sacrificed here after failing an attempt to take over the Kona and Kohala regions of Hawai'i. He had sent Kauhi, an informant, to see what sort of resistance might be expected, but the Hawaiian warriors hid from the Maui spy, who then erroneously assumed there were few fighting men in Kona. The defeat left Kauakahioka'ōkā and Kapapakō, the legendary black and white dogs of Kamalālāwalu, in the form of stone features on the temple platform, still waiting for their sacrificed master. The *heiau* measures approximately 100 by 150 feet with walls six to eleven feet in height, its *ma kai* side washed by the sea at high tide.

Hāpaiali'i (elevating chief) Heiau and an ancient house site stand just north of Ke'ekū Heiau. Some say Hāpaiali'i is older than Ke'ekū Heiau while others say it was built by Kamehameha I about 1782.

Beyond the lagoon is Pāokamenehune, a 3,900-foot breakwater said to have been constructed by the night-working *menehune* (legendary race of small people or elemental beings). Once enclosing the entire bay, the structure is also credited to Chief Kaleikini, who, legend tells, built Pāokamenehune with the help of supernatural powers.

Kapuanoni Heiau, a walled stone enclosure on Kahalu'u

A petroglyph at Kahalu'u depicts Maui chief Kamalālāwalu who, according to tradition, was beheaded and offered as a sacrifice at Ke'ekū Heiau. This and other petroglyphs at Keauhou are submerged at high tide.

Bay, was a temple dedicated to the increase of fish and food supply. The *heiau* was built by Kalani'ōpu'u. Beside it is Pohookapō, a sacred bathing tidepool for royalty, and a canoe-landing beach. Today this is a popular snorkeling area.

Not far from the canoe landing are two *kū'ula* stones, named Kanaio and 'Ulupalakua. These two fishgods were originally brought over by canoe from Maui in 1751. They watch over the Po'o Hawai'i Pond, also known as the King's Pond. This pool was sacred and reserved for *ali'i* families and *kāhuna*. It is said that bad luck will befall anyone who takes fish from this pond. Keauhou remained a favorite summer retreat for the royalty even after the capital moved to Lahaina and then to Honolulu. Keauhou means "new era."

Other points of interest are fresh water springs, a fertility pit, and the homesite of legendary *mo'o* twins, prophetic lizard goddesses. Part of the complex that is not on the Keauhou Beach Hotel property is the Lonoikamakahiki Residence on the private grounds of the nearby Surf and Racquet Club. Across Ali'i Drive, also on private property, are the overgrown Kona Gardens, a former archaeological park with at least one temple ruin, Papakōhōlua Heiau, and other ancient sites. At the time of writing, this area is slated for development.

The Keauhou Beach Hotel has artifacts on display in the lobby and provides guests with an informative map of the ancient sites on the hotel grounds. Regular tours of the site complex are offered. Call the hotel for tour reservations. (12/1-34; 27/2; 32/37, 39, 42; 37/104; 43/71-79 ).

> *Keauhou i ka 'ihi kapu.*
> Keauhou, where strict *kapu* were observed.
>
> *(Keauhou, Kona. This was the place where many*
> *of the highest chiefs resided and where*
> *Kamehameha III was born.)*
> —Hawaiian saying (35/181)

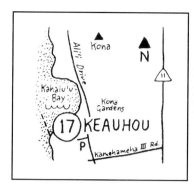

IV.17~LOCATION: On the grounds of Keauhou Beach Hotel, 78-6740 Ali'i Drive, Kona (Tel: 322-2727).

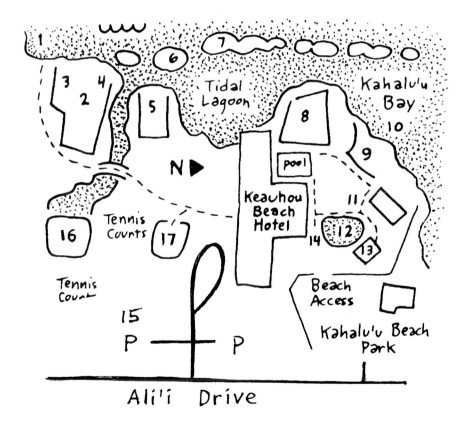

Keauhou sites: 1. Petroglyphs, 2. Ke'ekū Heiau, 3. Kauakahi'oka'ōkā, 4. Kapapakō, 5. Hāpaiali'i, 6. Kaluaokeli'i Cavern (named for a legendary shark), 7. Pāokamenehune, 8. Kapuanoni Heiau, 9. Canoe landing, 10. Pohookapō (sacred *ali'i* bathing pool), 11. Ku'ula stones, 12. Po'o Hawai'i (King's) Pond, 13. King Kalākaua's homesite, 14. *Ki'i*, 15. PunaWai Springs, 16. Legendary homesite of *mo'o* twins, 17. legendary Fertility Pit.

## IV.18 Ku'emanu Heiau
*Terraced stone platform*

This temple foundation is reputed to be a site where *ali'i* once offered prayers for good surfing conditions. Kahalu'u Bay, beside which the *heiau* stands, was a favorite *ali'i* surfing beach. An ancient brackish pool at the edge of the compound was where chiefs rinsed the salt from their bodies after surfing, and a well-spring known as Waiku'i can still be seen. A tiny missionary church, St. Peter's Catholic Church, is built over the former pool, *kāhuna* residence, and canoe shed area, just beyond the well. It was not uncommon for missionaries to build their churches on older sacred sites.

The well-constructed temple platform is built from large waterworn stones. Its main terrace slopes slightly and the upper terrace, five feet above the main platform, contains two five-foot-deep pits at its north end as well as a *luapa'ū* (a bone or refuse pit associated with *luakini heiau*).

The entire *heiau* precinct lies between *Ali'i* Drive and the ocean, measuring 90 feet by 237 feet. Ku'emanu Heiau was likely connected to the other sacred structures of nearby Keauhou complex. A seven-mile stretch of the Kona coast, of which this area is a part, was considered one of the most revered and sacred places on the Island of Hawai'i with more than two-dozen known *heiau* structures. (37/120; 43/67-70; 44/43)

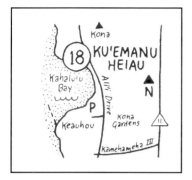

IV.18~LOCATION: Just north of Kahalu'u Beach Park on Ali'i Drive beside St. Peter's Church in Kona.

## IV.19 Ahu'ena Heiau

*Stone platform with restored thatched structures, wooden images, and canoe landing*

The name Ahu'ena means "hill of fire" or "red-hot heap," and it is the site of a fifteenth century *heiau luakini*. In 1812, after uniting the Hawaiian Islands, Kamehameha I retired to adjacent Kamakahonu (the turtle eye), where he put away the war god, Kūkā'ilimoku, and rededicated Ahu'ena Heiau to Lono, protector god of peace, agriculture, and prosperity. Ahu'ena precinct served as the place where Kamehameha's son, Liholiho, was instructed in the ways of a high chief. Following Kamehameha's death, Ahu'ena was destroyed when the *kapu* system was rejected by his successor, Liholiho, Kamehameha II.

The restored *heiau* has a large *hale mana* (place of spiritual power), a wicker *lele* (altar), an *'anu'u* tower and several wooden *ki'i* (carved figures). The carved image with the plover bird on its head is a god of war. A sacred drum called Apahou, decorated with human teeth, was housed here at Ahu'ena. Pigs, bananas, coconuts, and men were offered as sacrifices at *luakini heiau*.

Although the original platform of the *heiau* extended beyond the modern pier, Ahu'ena was carefully restored at a somewhat smaller size in 1975, at the cost of a quarter-million dollars. A National Historic Landmark, it is visible from the pier or can be approached from the King Kamehameha Kona Beach Hotel. Informational signs are provided at the site and the hotel offers daily tours at 1:30 P.M. (14/60; 16/122-123; 24/1-19; 26/166; 37/6; 43/43-47; 44/40-42)

IV.19~LOCATION: King Kamehameha Kona Beach Hotel, 75-5660 Palani Road, Kailua-Kona (Tel: 329-2911).

𝟛𝟙❂❂𝟛𝟙❂❂𝟛𝟙❂❂

Ahu'ena Heiau has been restored to look much like it did to Captain von Kotzebue and the crew of his Russian ship when they visited Hawai'i in 1816. (Based on an etching by ship artist, Ludwig Choris.)

## IV.20 Kaloko-Honokōhau
### National Historical Park
*Rock enclosures and platforms, fishponds,* hōlua *slide, petroglyphs, and burial sites*

Kaloko Fishpond and Honokōhau complex are the remnants of an active ancient Hawaiian community along the dry region of the Kona coast. With two major fishponds and a fishtrap, at least two *heiau*, numerous house ruins, petroglyphs, a *hōlua* slide, and many burial places, the area provides valuable indications of old Hawaiian settlement patterns. The complex has been designated a National Historical Park.

At the upper end of the park is Kaloko Fishpond, a brackish-water pond with a massive manmade seawall. The pond is presently being restored by the National Parks Service to its original productive condition. (Kamehameha I is presumed by some to be buried in this area. Chiefs were often buried in secret places in order to preserve *mana* (spiritual power) from adversaries. Kamehameha's remains have never been found.) Five endangered plant and animal species have been identified at the pond site and conservation measures have been taken by the Park Service. To the south of Kaloko is 'Aimakapā Fishpond, which is in disuse and partially silted over. 'Ai'ōpio Fishtrap at the southwestern corner of the park is one of the few remaining traps of its kind in Hawai'i and is best seen at low tide.

Also in the southern area of the park are the two *heiau*, one of which stands beside the fishtrap and is called Pu'uoina. This *heiau* has been stabilized by the Park Service. Outside of the park and just across the harbor to the south on Noio Point is Makaopi'o Heiau, with two impressive upright stones, and Hale o Lono, which overlooks Honokōhau Bay. The federal government is trying to acquire this land from the state to preserve these sites and include them in the park.

The National Historical Park was established in 1978 to preserve traditional native Hawaiian sites and to demonstrate historic land-use patterns. Future plans include building an underground visitors center and establishing interpretive trails throughout the park.

For specific directions to sites within the park, visitors should contact the Kaloko-Honokōhau National Historical Park headquarters. Guided tours of portions of the park are provided by arrangement only. An informational brochure is available. The park is open daily from 7:30 A.M. to 3:30 P.M. The park office is located in the Kaloko Industrial Park directly across Ka'ahumanu Highway 19, and is open 7:30 A.M. to 4 P.M., Monday through Friday. (14/65; 26/167-168; 37/49, 77-78; 39; 41/104-110)

Inquiries should be addressed to the National Park Service, 73-4786 Kanalani Street, #14, Kailua-Kona, HI 96740 (Tel: 329-6881).

*Hōlua* stone ramp used by *ali'i* in sledding competitions at Kaloko-Honokōhau.

IV.20~LOCATION:   One access road into the park is off Highway 19, 3.5 miles south of  Keāhole Airport and 3.4 miles north of Kailua-Kona, directly across from Kaloko Industrial Park.  It is an unmarked dirt road heading *ma kai* (toward the ocean). Another entrance is at  Honokōhau harbor, off the harbor access road.

Entrance to petroglyph field at Ka'ūpūlehu in North Kona.

## IV.21 Ka'ūpūlehu

*Petroglyphs, fishponds,* hōlua, *and house sites.*

Known as Manuahi (fire bird) in the old days, the present land division, which was home to an ancient Kona fishing village, is now called Kaʻūpūlehu (the roasted breadfruit), possibly a contraction of Kaimupūlehuakeakua (the roasting oven of the gods) Its name was changed following the last eruption of Hualālai in 1801, when, according to local tradition, Pele became jealous of Kamehameha the Great's prosperous land and sea resources in this area. The volcano goddess started a lava flow from a vent at the 6,000-foot elevation, which set out to consume all *aku* and *awa* fish as well as all the breadfruit in the district. Pele's anger was not quelled until Kamehameha offered sacrifices at the advice of a *kāula* (seer) of Pele.

An older tradition speaks of two girls, Pāhinahina and Kolomuʻo, who were roasting breadfruit when Pele came upon them, and only Pāhinahina showed *aloha* by offering the goddess some of her cooking. Later that night, Hualālai erupted, destroying Huʻehuʻe village where the girls lived, sparing only the home of Pāhinahina.

Isaac Davis, a late-eighteenth-century seaman once serving on the *Fair American*, noted that Kaʻūpūlehu had a large bay. (Everyone on board the *Fair American*, except for Davis, was killed by Hawaiians. He had fought so bravely that his life was spared. The attack on the ship's company was made in retaliation for the flogging of a chief by a Captain Metcalf of the *Eleanora* just a few days earlier. As Metcalf's son was captain of the *Fair American*, Metcalf thus inadvertently brought about his son's death. The crew of the *Fair American* is believed to be buried in the Kaʻūpūlehu area. Isaac Davis subsequently became a trusted advisor of Kamehameha I and died in Honolulu in 1810.) Today, the bay is relatively small, indicating that the 1801 lava flow may have added new land, thus decreasing its expanse to what we see now. The bay is called Kahuwai, which means "water tender."

In 1959, Johnno Jackson determined to reconstruct the ancient village settlement of Kaʻūpūlehu to accomodate guests in a small, isolated resort, accessible only by sea. Kona Village Resort, as it is now known, later built a private air strip that was eventually replaced in the 1970s with an access road. The concept of this resort at Kaʻūpūlehu is what makes it such a unique place. Each guest house is built to resemble a Polynesian *hale*, be it Hawaiian, Samoan, Tahitian, Maori, or New Caledonian. Known for its "no phones, radios, or television" vacations, the resort does not replicate the original fourteenth-century fishing village but it does provide a more appropriate setting than is often the case for viewing ancient sites.

Some of the ancient house sites have modern *hale* built over them while others have been left as mere foundation walls or platforms for display purposes. Part of a *hōlua* (sled) ramp is preserved at the edge of the resort where *ali'i* (chiefs) challenged each other in sledding contests. The village fishponds are presently being restored and provide guests with the diversion of pole fishing for tilapia.

However, it is the fifteen-acre petroglyph field that is of special interest. The extent and uniqueness of the Ka'ūpūlehu petroglyphs have only recently been confirmed. Clearing and surveying of the *ki'i pōhaku* (pictures in stone) have revealed images that are found nowhere else in Hawai'i—or the world, for that matter. Such petroglyphs include the so-called surfing fisherman and the head-to-head twins. Also, very elaborate kite

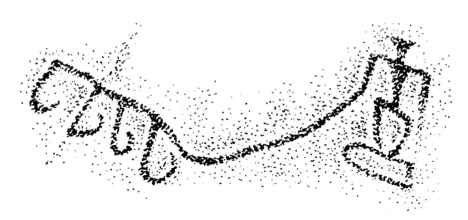

An unusual petroglyph of a "surfing fisherman" is found in the vicinity of the former Kona fishing village of Ka'ūpūlehu. A human figure standing upon what appears to be a surfboard casts a line with four fish hooks on it out in front of his board.

designs are unique to this field. The most unusual aspect of this site is the large number of Hawaiian sail motifs pecked into the smooth *pāhoehoe* lava. No place else on the Big Island or in the Hawaiian archipelago do so many sail pictures exist side by side, and yet only the sail, without the hull of the canoe, seems to appear. Kona Village Resort uses the one-of-a-kind double-crab-claw sail petroglyph image found at this site as its trademark.

A brochure with a map of the petroglyph field is available to guests of the resort for self-guided tours. Biweekly historic tours are offered to guests as well as to the general public by reservation only. Call the resort for days and times. A more general tour of the resort is given daily, Monday through Friday, at 11 A.M., also by reservation (Tel: 325-5555). (37/52-53, 96)

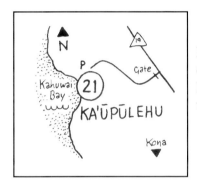

IV.21~LOCATION: Five miles north of Keāhole Airport off Queen Ka'ahumanu Highway (Route 19), and two miles from entrance checkpoint.

Wooden *ki'i* at Ka'ūpūlehu, North Kona.

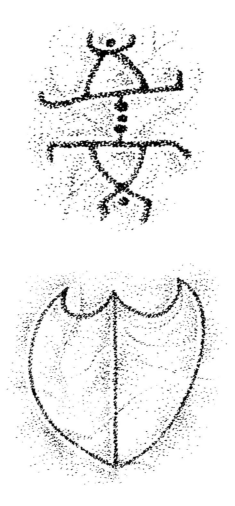

At Ka'ūpūlehu is a rare "twins" petroglyph. Placed head-to-head, the triangular human figures have a *piko* point between the two heads and between each pair of legs. The word *piko* refers to the navel, the genitals, and to blood relatives.

The unique "double sail" petroglyph is found within a petroglyph field that contains more sail images than any other single site in the Hawaiian Islands.

Ancient house site at Ka'ūpūlehu in Kona.

Fishing shrine at 'Anaeho'omalu in Kohala.

# V Kohala

From the barren lava fields of Kanikū (upright sound) in South Kohala to the windy mountain heights and weather-beaten valleys of North Kohala, this region of the Big Island has many sites that attest to its ancient history.

In South Kohala, there are many fishponds and settlements where the vast lava flows of former times meet the sea. Extensive clusters of petroglyphs are etched into the stone ground beside ancient trails. Stone-walled shelters constructed as windbreaks against the strong ʻĀpaʻapaʻa wind can be found throughout this area as well as in North Kona. There are linear rock shelters, L-shaped, V-shaped, and the most common, C-shaped shelters. Some sites that constitute remnants of early settlements have been incorporated into parks within hotel grounds and are open to the public.

Puʻukoholā Heiau National Historic Site in South Kohala played a very important role in the religious and political life of late prehistoric and early historic Hawaiʻi. Its impressive stone platform was the last major Hawaiian temple to be built in the islands. From Puʻukoholā north along the coast are the ruins of many small agricultural and fishing settlements, the most interesting of which is Lapakahi, a stabilized ancient village and State Historical Park. Near the northernmost end of Hawaiʻi Island is Kamehameha I Birthplace State Memorial and the ancient Moʻokini Heiau. This *heiau*, along with its sister temple, Wahaʻula (Site II.11, pg.71), on almost the exact opposite end of the island in Puna, is said to have been dedicated by the Polynesian *kahuna* Pāʻao between the tenth and thirteenth centuries A.D. Moʻokini Heiau has an oral tradition that claims an even earlier origin to about the fifth century A.D.

Other temples in the North Kohala district that are not easily accessible are Kukuipahu Heiau, associated with the *kahuna* Kamapiʻikai and said to have Tahitian or Marquesan architectural influences; Kuapālaha Heiau, which overlooks Kēōkea Bay; Hale o Kā'ili, a family *heiau* of Kamehameha I; and Kapālama Heiau, with its sacrificial *holehole* (to peel, strip off) stone.

Also in North Kohala is the legendary *pōhaku* (stone) known as Kamehameha Rock. Carried miles up from the coast, this stone is a monument not only to the first king's great physical strength, but most of all to a spiritual strength and greatness seen throughout ancient Hawaiian culture.

> *Ipu lei Kohala na ka Moa'e kū.*
> Kohala is like a wreath container for the (strong) Moa'e breeze.

> *(Kohala is a windy place.)*
> —Hawaiian saying (35/136)

A simple line petroglyph depicting a possible mother and son is likely of earlier origin than figures carved with outlines, triangular torso, and muscles. Puakō, Kohala.

## Kohala Region Sites

22. 'Anaeho'omalu
23. Kalāhuipua'a
24. Puakō Petroglyphs
25. Pu'ukoholā Heiau (National Historic Site)
26. Lapakahi (State Historical Park)
27. Kamehameha I Birthplace (State Memorial)
28. Mo'okini Heiau
29. Kamehameha Rock

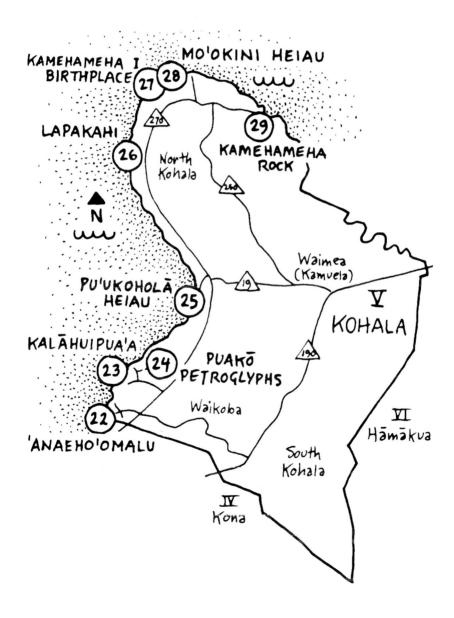

## V.22 'Anaeho'omalu

*Fishponds, rock enclosures, trail and petroglyphs*

The 'Anaeho'omalu Bay area has two important fishponds that supplied the local *ali'i* families of the region with fresh mullet. *'Anae* is the Hawaiian word for "mullet" and *ho'omalu* means "protected." Ku'uali'i and Kahapapa Fishponds are maintained as active ponds within the resort setting of the Royal Waikoloan Hotel. A *mākāhā* (sluice gate) separates the two ponds from each other and a second gate connects Kahapapa with the bay. Numerous anchialine ponds, with unique miniature red shrimp populations, rise and fall with the tides and are protected in this area. Signs providing information about the ponds are found along paved walkways.

*Ma uka* (toward the mountains) of Ku'uali'i Fishpond are the restored rock enclosures of a likely housesite and fishing shrine. The one enclosure, called a *hale noa*, is where husband and wife could meet together. The nearby *mua* is the men's eating house and *kapu* to women. Between the two structures lies a coral pile indicating a place of ritual offering. Here a *kia'i loko*, "pond keeper," would pray for plenty to Kū'ulakai, god of fishponds, and his wife, Hinapukui'a. Upright *kū'ula pōhaku* (sacred stones dedicated to fishing) are also at the site.

The other important site in the 'Anaeho'omalu area is the extensive Waikoloa Petroglyph Preserve in the midst of the Waikoloa Golf Course. Carvings are found on some of the smoother *pāhoehoe* lava formations. The King's Highway, built in the nineteenth century over the older Ala Māmalahoa trail, can be seen cutting across the lava beds and weaving in between the petroglyph images. Dotting the landscape beside the trail are C-shaped stone breakwalls, used by early travelers as shelters against the prevailing winds.

Two of the most common forms of petroglyph carvings at this site are the *puka* or *lua*, which appear as dots, cup marks, or holes, and the ring or circle carvings. The first interpretation of these markings by a westerner was made by the Reverend William Ellis in the early nineteenth century, when he suggested they stood for the number of times an individual (dot) circumambulated the island (ring). Semicircles were thought to represent partial journeys. It is known, however, that the *piko* (umbilical cord stump) of a newborn child was wrapped in tapa cloth, placed in such a *lua*, and covered with a stone in order to absorb *mana* (spiritual power) from the cosmos. If overnight the *piko* disappeared, the child in question would, according to one legend, become a thief because the Great Rat was then thought to have influence over him. Recent research has suggested that the circular carvings may represent male children while the semicircular forms may indicate female.

Other more recognizable carved images are human figures in various styles, canoes, a turtle, a crab claw, fishhooks, and even a nineteenth-century cowboy on horseback. (Ranch hands were imported from Mexico in the 1830s in order to teach Hawaiians cattle punching and help control the large herds of wild cattle that had multiplied since their introduction to the island in the 1790s.) Cowboys were called *paniolo* in Hawaiian. A stick-figure image of Lono, god of the Makahiki festival, can be seen amongst the other petroglyphs beside the old foot-worn Ala Māmalahoa trail. It is estimated that the earliest petroglyphs were done around 800 A.D., when the 'Anaeho'omalu region was first extensively settled.

A self-guiding map of the petroglyph field is available from the King's Shops or the Royal Waikoloan Hotel. Remember that the best viewing time for petroglyphs is in early morning or late afternoon. Please do not walk over image areas or harm the rock art in any way. (1/94; 8/48-49, 54; 10; 26/169; 27/6, 8; 32/37; 37/12)

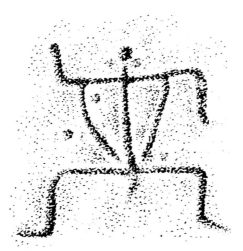

A petroglyph at ʻAnaehoʻomalu shows a deeply carved male stick figure with a shallow cut triangular body, an indication that the full torso may have been a later addition.

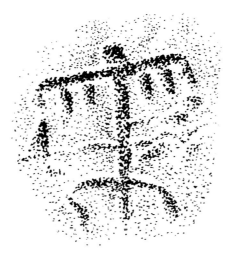

Lono, god of peace and abundance, was especially revered at the winter Makahiki festival. The sign of Lono, a cross-beam with hanging *kapa* (tapa) cloth, can be seen beside an ancient foot trail that goes through the Waikoloa Petroglyphs Preserve in Kohala.

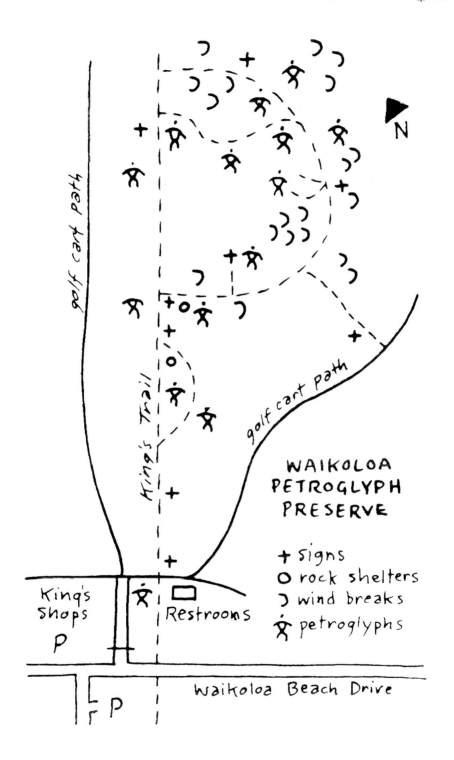

N

WAIKOLOA
PETROGLYPH
PRESERVE

+ signs
O rock shelters
⊃ wind breaks
⨉ petroglyphs

King's
Shops
P

Restrooms

Waikoloa Beach Drive

P

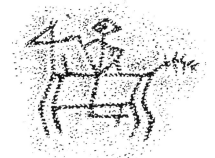

This petroglyph of a horseback rider at 'Anaeho'omalu, Kohala, records the early historic introduction of *paniolo* (cowboys) from Mexico to control the cattle population, which had become destructive to Big Island flora. Waikoloa Petroglyph Preserve at 'Anaeho'omalu displays hundreds of images carved in stone, as well as rock shelters and windbreaks along the old King's Trail.

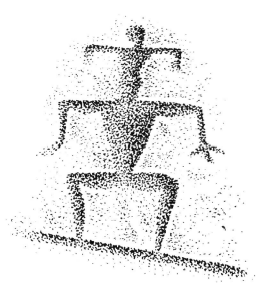

A surfer with an elaborate headdress, a guardian spirit, or a young rider on its head, can be found at 'Anaeho'omalu.

In early historic times new images such as introduced animals, words, ships, and this church found their way into the imagery of the petroglyph artists.

A petroglyph at 'Anaeho'omalu shows an old Hawaiian-style fishhook with an anvil-type lashing.

V.22~LOCATION: From Queen Ka'ahumanu Highway, Route 19 in South Kohala, *ma kai* (toward the sea) on Waikoloa Beach Drive and right into the King's Shops and petroglyph parking area. For fishpond parking, turn left on Pae Wa'a and proceed to public beach parking. Royal Waikoloan Hotel, P.O. Box 5000, Waikoloa, HI 96743 (Tel: 885-6789).

## V.23 Kalāhuipuaʻa

*Fishponds, petroglyphs, cave shelters, and house sites.*

The area known as Kalāhuipuaʻa (family of pigs) is centered around four ponds, the largest of which is Kalāhuipuaʻa Fishpond, still in use today.  Before 1500 A.D. the anchialine ponds were part of a six-hundred-acre brackish lagoon, and two beautiful *moʻo wahine* (female water beings)  were said to live in the large pond.  Pele, the volcano goddess, became jealous of the lovely water maidens and sent a destructive lava flow, known as the Kanikū flow, to divide the pond. Kanikū was also the name of one of the *moʻo* sisters and Kanimoe was her twin. Both were turned to stone by Pele.

Kalāhuipuaʻa pond is 4.6 acres in size and reaches a depth of eighteen feet in places.  A restored *mākāhā* (sluice gate) can be seen on the *ma kai* (seaward) side of the fishpond, and *ʻamaʻama* (mullet) and *awa* (milkfish) are the primary stock, along with shrimp.  Other fish that enter the shoreline ponds are *pāpio* (young ulua), *manini* (surgeon fish), *kākū* (barracuda), and *puhi* (moray eel).  As with most ancient Hawaiian fishponds, these ponds were under the control of the *aliʻi* (chiefs), and most of the fish were reserved for their consumption. Runners transported fish wrapped in wet *limu* (seaweed), over long distances, still fresh and wiggling to the chief's *hale* (house). These ponds belonged to Kamehameha the Great at one time.

Kalāhuipua'a also may have the meaning "abundant in food." Mullet filled this pond and were sometimes called *pua'a kai* (sea pig). Therefore, it is suggested that "an area abounding in mullet" is a likely intention in the word Kalāhuipua'a.

A paved trail leads around the ponds and along the coast to dozens of ancient sites. Of special interest is the historic preserve through which the Ala Loa or King's Trail passes. Here one finds natural lava tube cave shelters that were used by the Hawaiians from 1200-1700 A.D. Many of the caves have been excavated, revealing artifacts such as large fishhooks for catching shark, stone tools, and a canoe paddle. Petroglyphs, such as the dramatic helmeted warrior, can also be found in this area where the preserve, fishponds, and golf course meet.

Kalāhuipua'a complex is a historic preserve with many ancient features: 1) Kalāhuipua'a Trail leads through a lava field where ancient basalt tools were manufactured; 2) lava tube shelter cave; 3) petroglyph of helmeted warrior; 4) "Kūlia" Petroglyphs; 5) Hope'ala Pond; 6) Kalāhuipua'a Fishpond; 7) Keawanui canoe landing; 8) Waipuhi Pond; 9) Waipuhi Iki Pond; 10) *mākāhā*; 11) Ka'alopio Pond; 12) Manokū Pond; and 13) Eva Parker Woods Cottage Museum.

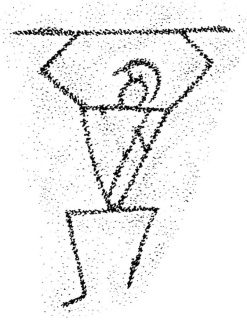

Close to the Ala Loa (long trail), or King's Trail, is the unusual "helmeted warrior" petroglyph. With spear raised in both hands over a crested feather helmet, the figure is carved in triangular-outline body type. A lava tube cave shelter can be visited in the Kalāhuiphua'a historic preserve.

The fishponds and historic preserve are featured sites within the grounds of the Mauna Lani Bay Resort and Golf Course. The Eva Parker Woods Cottage, at the resort, is a tiny museum featuring replica artifacts such as bone fishhooks, weapons, wooden calabashes, and items excavated from forty nearby shelter and burial caves. The Mauna Lani Resort prints an informative self-guiding map of the Kalāhuipua'a 'ili (small land division) that it makes available to its guests. Check with the resort for museum hours and other cultural activities. (1/94: 10; 28/167-175; 37/73; 44/75)

V.23~LOCATION: Off Queen Ka'ahumanu Highway, *ma kai* on Mauna Lani Drive to the public parking area. Mauna Lani Resort, P.O. Box 4959, HRC 2, Kohala, HI 96743 (Tel: 885-6622).

# V.24 Puakō Petroglyphs
*Petroglyph field*

Puakō Petroglyph Archaeological Preserve, a registered historic place, has petroglyphs believed to have been carved between 1000 and 1800 A.D. (The age is estimated by the simple stick-figure style, and is not certain.) Puakō has over three thousand petroglyphs, an unusually large concentration of carvings.

Profile figures are rare in Hawaiian petroglyphs. However, this crouching form is similar to an image found in Moanalua on Oʻahu (now in the BIshop Museum), which in turn bears a resemblance to Polynesian "birdman" petroglyphs on Easter Island. (17.32-24; 27/58-62)

Many of the petroglyphs are *puka* or *lua*, cup marks and dots connected to the postbirth ritual of placing the *piko* (umbilical cord stump) of a child in the carved hole with a rock over the top. It was believed that this would result in helpful *mana* (spiritual power) from the cosmos nourishing the child.

There are also many human figures depicted at Puakō. Perhaps the most interesting is a series of thirty figures lined up head to foot and believed to be a column of marching warriors. Chiefs, somewhat larger in size, stand off to the side. However, these petroglyphs might also indicate a particular family lineage. These figures lie close to Ka'eo (winning) Trail. (Of note is that Keōua, the last relative standing in the way of Kamehameha I's takeover of Hawai'i Island, was said to be buried here at Paniau, Puakō, after Kamehameha had him sacrificed at nearby Pu'ukoholā Heiau.)

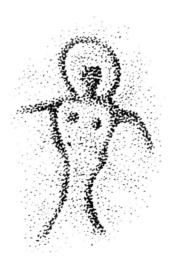

A female figure with "halo," at Puakō Petroglyph Preserve.

At the beginning of the trail to the preserve, replica petroglyphs have been provided for those who wish to make rubbings. However, rubbings from authentic petroglyphs are prohibited because of the destruction the process causes to the stone images. Just less than one mile of trail will lead you to the Puakō petroglyph field where a viewing platform was recently installed. Please do not walk out onto the petroglyphs. Viewing is best in early morning or late afternoon light. (1/94; 8/28-34, 42-47; 26/170; 27/59, 75; 32/35-37; 37/191)

V.24~LOCATION: From Queen Ka'ahumanu Highway take Mauna Lani Drive *ma kai* (towards the sea) to North Kanikū Drive, following signs to Puakō Petroglyphs Archaeological Preserve. Parking is available at Holoholokai Beach Park. Mālama Trail, .7 miles, leads to the site. Open 6:30 A.M. to 7 P.M.

A birthing scene at Puakō shows two adult figures, a male and a female, and two infants, male and female. The males are of the triangular and muscled body type, with their surfaces thoroughly pecked out. The females are outline figures with the torsos open at the bottom. A *piko* point indicates the birth canal of the adult female.

## V.25 Puʻukoholā Heiau
National Historic Site
*Enclosed stone structures*, pōhaku, *and other ruins.*

    Puʻukoholā Heiau is the central feature of this National Historic Site established in 1972 on seventy-seven acres of Kohala coastland.  Also within the historic park are Mailekini Heiau, Hale o Kapuni Heiau site, a *pōhaku* (stone) leaning post, and the house site of John Young, a trusted western advisor to Kamehameha the Great.

    Begun in 1790, Puʻukoholā was the last major *heiau* built in Hawaiʻi. It was prophesied by the *kahuna* (priest) Kapoukahi of Kauaʻi that Kamehameha would fulfill his destiny only if he built a *luakini* (human sacrifice) *heiau* atop Puʻukoholā, "whale hill." Built on what is believed to have been an older temple site, the renovated *heiau* was dedicated to Kūkāʻilimoku, the family war god of Kamehameha, and was completed within a year.  The red waterworn stones for the *heiau* were passed from hand to hand over a distance of fourteen miles from Pololū Valley. Keliʻimaikaʻi, Kamehameha's highborn brother, presided over the construction of the temple but was restricted from doing any of the work in order that one *aliʻi* should remain pure.  Once when

Keli'imaika'i picked up a stone, Kamehameha quickly took it from him and had it taken out to sea beyond the horizon and dropped overboard. Other island chiefs feared the prophecy of Kapoukahi and went to war against Kamehameha. It was at this time that the battle of Kepūwaha'ula'ula, "red-mouthed cannon," took place off the coast of Waipi'o Valley to the north (pg. 152). From the south, an attack was made by Keōua, cousin of Kamehameha. When Pu'ukoholā Heiau was finally completed, Kamehameha "invited" his rival cousin Keōua to the opening ceremony of the temple, which in effect required the latter to attend but surely meant his death. Apparently knowing that he would be offered as the principal sacrifice, tradition tells that Keōua cut off the head of his penis while enroute to Pu'ukoholā, thus making himself a less-than-perfect offering. Nevertheless, Keōua and his top aides were slain and offered at the *heiau*. Some say that the spoiling of the sacrifice is the reason that Kamehameha was never able to conquer Kaua'i and Ni'ihau. However, Kamehameha had subdued Maui, Moloka'i, and Lāna'i by 1794. In 1795, he took O'ahu, and in 1810 even Kaua'i had reached an agreement to become a part of the new Hawaiian kingdom under the rule of its first monarch. The prophecy of Kapoukahi had been fulfilled; Pu'ukoholā Heiau had been built and Kamehameha had become ruler of the Hawaiian Islands.

In August 1991, a healing ceremony was held at Pu'ukoholā for members of the Hawaiian community celebrating the 200th anniversary of the temple's dedication. Prayers, chants, and *ho'okupu* (gifts) were offered by descendants of native Hawaiians who had taken part in the death of Keōua in an effort to heal the wounds and bad feelings created by the sacrifice two centuries before.

Pu'ukoholā Heiau, which is positioned on the edge of a small plateau 150 feet above sea level and 400 feet east of the bay, is constructed of carefully selected *'alā* (waterworn) stones. Its thick walls on the north, east, and south sides protect the raised main platform from view, and though the west side is completely open, its height prohibits views of any proceedings within the *heiau*. One-third of the interior is occupied by a large platform containing several divisions, which may indicate the position of original *hale* (house) structures. The *luapa'ū* (bone pit) and *lele* (altar) area are believed to be located near the western edge of the platform. The public is not permitted to enter Pu'ukoholā Heiau. Please respect this site.

Mailekini, literally meaning "many *maile* vines," is a prehistoric *heiau* used by the ancestors of Kamehameha. Just down the hill, 170 feet to the west of Puʻukoholā Heiau, this older temple structure was at one time covered with many different *kiʻi* (wooden images). However, Mailekini Heiau was not a *luakini* temple and no human sacrifices were offered to its gods. During historic times, John Young, an advisor to Kamehameha I, converted it into a fort in order to better protect the Kawaihae area.

Puʻukoholā Heiau National Historical Site is perhaps the most important temple complex of late prehistoric and early historic times in Hawaiʻi. It is from here that Kamehameha the Great established and confirmed the *mana* (spiritual power) necessary for his conquest of the Hawaiian Islands. Three *heiau* sites are in close proximity to each other here.

Hale o Kapuni is a third *heiau* site within the park boundaries but is entirely submerged just offshore. There are no plans for the excavation of this *heiau*, which was dedicated to shark gods. As representatives of these gods, sharks would circle the island-like temple platform, devouring offerings placed there for them. The high chief Alapa'ikūpalupalumanō would watch the ritual feeding from a *pōhaku* (stone) leaning post on shore.

An early historic ruin, the first western-style house in Hawai'i is the John Young House Site, also located in the park. A rock-and-mortar structure, it was home to a stranded British sailor serving on the *Eleanora*. He was left at Kealakekua Bay after a *kapu* (taboo) had been placed on his ship due to an earlier incident at Ka'ūpūlehu (pg. 111). John Young was called Olohana (after the English mariners' expression "all hands") by Kamehameha I, and became a trusted advisor to the king. He married the niece of Kamehameha, Ka'oana'eha, and served as governor of the island of Hawai'i from 1802 to 1814. His granddaughter, Queen Emma, was the wife of Kamehameha IV. Young died in 1835 and was entombed as an *ali'i* in the Royal Mausoleum in Honolulu.

Mailekini Heiau at Pu'ukoholā Heiau National Historic Site in Kohala.

Rangers at the Pu'ukoholā Heiau National Historic Site provide visitors with an orientation talk, and a small informative brochure is available to help guide one to the various ancient sites. Entrance to the park is free of charge. Hours are 7:30 A.M. to 4 P.M. daily. (1/94-95; 2/6-28; 11/96 99/ 14/56-57, 68-69; 16/17; 26/175; 37/199-200; 43/164-171)

Pōkaku "leaning post" at Pu'ukoholā Heiau National Historic Site.

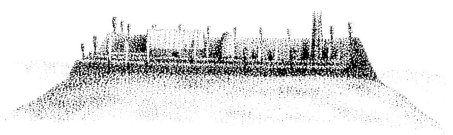

Pu'ukoholā Heiau was completed by Kamehameha the Great as a *luakini heiau* in 1791. Dedicated to the war god, Kūkā'ilimoku, the temple was specifically constructed for the purpose of increasing the *mana* and political power of Kamehameha. Though a stone foundation and outer rock walls are now all that remain, a *hale mana, hale pahu, 'anu'u* (oracle tower), and *akua ki'i*, as well as other religious structures, would have completed the temple architecture.

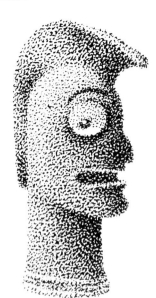

Kūkā'ilimoku, the fearsome war aspect of the god Kū, was given to Kamehameha the Great by his uncle, Big Island chief Kalani'ōpu'u, before his death. With this deity at his side, Kamehameha eventually rose to become the most powerful chief in all Hawai'i. Standing more than two feet tall, the feathered god had eyes of pearl shell and lips lined with ninety-four dog teeth. Red 'i'iwi feathers covered the ancient bust, yellow ō'ō feathers edged the lower neck and crowned the upper crest. This particular feather image was hidden for many years in a cave in Kona. It was sold to Bishop Museum in 1895. (15/503-504). "It is said that at times, in the heat of battle, it uttered cries which were heard above the clash of arms."—David Kalākaua (18/44)

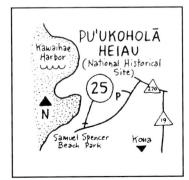

V.25~LOCATION: *Ma kai* (toward the sea) of Akoni Pule Highway, Star Route 270, just past the junction of Kawaihae Road (19) and Queen Ka'ahumanu Highway. Pu'ukoholā Heiau National Historic Site, Box 44340, Kawaihae, HI 96743 (Tel: 882-7218).

## V.26 Lapakahi
State Historical Park
*Stone platforms, rock enclosures,* heiau, *burial sites,* pōhaku, *and ancient artifacts.*

Lapakahi is a 600-year-old partially restored fishing and farming village along the North Kohala coastline. One of the first archaeological surveys to analyze an entire *ahupua'a* (land division extending from mountains to sea) was carried out here by the University of Hawai'i in the 1960s and 1970s. Now a State Historical Park, Lapakahi provides a unique glimpse into the community life of an ancient Hawaiian settlement that worked both the land and the sea.

A stone-lined footpath connects the coastal region with the upland agricultural fields. Residential sites, rock shelters, and burial platforms are found in both areas. The park is focused around the coastal sites such as fishing shrines, canoe sheds, and salt pans. This village was apparently home to commoners involved in the hard work of daily existence. Only a small number of *ali'i* (chiefs) are believed to have lived under these conditions at Lapakahi.

The park is set up as a family-oriented educational experience with many hands-on activities, especially Hawaiian games such as *'ō'ō ihe* (spear throwing), *'ulu maika* (disc rolling), *kōnane* (a kind of checkers), *pala'ie* (loop and ball), and *moa pahe'e* (dart sliding). A free brochure indicating two dozen ancient sites along the park trail is available. Hours are 8 A.M. to 4 P.M. daily; admission is free. (1/94; 10/29-31; 14/63-64; 26/177-78; 33; 37/129; 44/74)

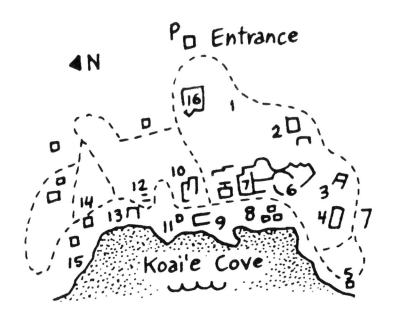

Lapakahi in North Kohala, is open to visitors as a State Historical Park with such ancient features as: 1) multiple platform burial sites; 2) house and burial sites; 3) canoe shed; 4) early historic house; 5) *ko'a* (fishing shrine); 6) well; 7) house site; 8) salt pans; 9) canoe shed or house site; 10) *heiau*; 11) *ko'a*; 12) salt pans; 13) house site; 14) fire pit; 15) *kōnane* (game stone); and 16) rock shelters.

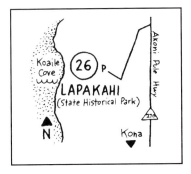

V.26~LOCATION: *Ma kai* (toward the sea) of Akoni Pule Highway, Star Route 270, twelve miles north of Kawaihae. Lapakahi State Historical Park, Box 100, Kapa'au, HI 96755 (Tel: 889-5566).

# V.27 Kamehameha I Birthplace
State Memorial
*Rock wall enclosure*

Kamehameha the Great is believed to have been born here at Kāpakai, Kokoiki, in 1758. According to chants, he was then taken to nearby Moʻokini Heiau for his postbirth ritual. Prophecy had already spoken of this child, "the lone one" or "the lonely one," as having a future of greatness, becoming the first and only chief to unite the entire Hawaiian Islands. As a young child, he was taken to Waipiʻo Valley in order to hide him from the ruling chief of Hawaiʻi who feared the prophecy.

The rock wall enclosure was renovated by volunteers from the nearby Coast Guard station and, although little is to be seen at the site besides the surrounding natural beauty, a plaque and Hawaiʻi Visitors Bureau sign indicate its significance as the birthplace of the first Kamehameha.

Kamehameha I Birthplace State Memorial, Moʻokini Heiau, and Kukuipahu Heiau, along with other sites in Māhukona, have recently been designated part of the Kohala Historical Sites State Monument for their cultural and historical significance. (10/33-34; 14/58; 44/73)

V.27~LOCATION: Two miles *ma kai* of Akoni Pule Highway 270, to 'Upolu Airport, then left along the dirt road past Mo'okini Heiau .4 miles. Look for a Hawai'i Visitors Bureau sign, and the state memorial will be *ma uka*. (Road is impassible in wet weather.)

Kamehameha the Great
1758-1819

## V.28 Moʻokini Heiau

*Large stone platform and walled enclosures,* pōhaku

Moʻokini Heiau is an extremely impressive ancient site within a secluded coastal setting. The architectural features of this prehistoric temple include enclosure walls of basalt ʻalā (water-worn) stones. Some of the walls reach a height of thirty feet. The longest part of the enclosure extends some 267 feet in length by 37 feet in width.

One of the smaller enclosures within this *luakini heiau* (temple of human sacrifice) is the *aliʻi nui* shelter. Once enclosed by an ʻōhiʻa wood and *pili* grass structure, this area was where the ruling chiefs prayed, fasted, and offered human sacrifices. A scalloped altar is the focal point of the *heiau* and a trademark of Pāʻao, a *kahuna* from Kahiki who introduced a powerful religio-political order to the islands between the tenth and thirteenth centuries. The customary offering made at the altar today is a closed *ʻieʻie lei*, made from a vine that grows in the mountains of Kohala and is sacred to the god of Moʻokini Heiau, Kū. In the past, human sacrifices were readied for offering at Pōhaku Holchole Kānaka (stone [for] stripping human [flesh]), a large dishlike stone in front of the *heiau*. It is said that it was here that the flesh was removed from sacrificial victims and the bones made into fishhooks or other objects. A striking view of the Haleakalā side of Maui is visible from this spot on a clear day.

According to traditional genealogical chants of the Mo'okini family, this *heiau* was built around 480 A.D. It is more generally believed, however that at least a part of the structure was built when Pā'ao, who is also considered the architect of Waha'ula Heiau on the south coast (Site II.11, pg. 71), arrived in Hawai'i and established a new order of worship and rulership. The Mo'okini oral history speaks of Pā'ao merely raising the walls of the *heiau* from their original height of six feet to their present thirty-foot height. The chants also speak of 15,000 to 18,000 men building the stone structure in one night by passing rocks, hand to hand, fourteen miles from Pololū Valley. If a stone was dropped, it was left where it lay; therefore, a trail of scattered rocks can be seen between Pololū and Mo'okini.

Archaeologists are uncomfortable with the traditional history as it is expressed in the family chants, believing the late fifth century to be an unjustifiably early date. According to these chants, however, the original construction of the *heiau* was overseen by *kahuna nui* Kuamo'o Mo'okini. Mo'okini means "many lineages" and, according to Leimomi Mo'okini Lum, who currently carries the priestly responsibilities for the temple, the *heiau* has had an unbroken line of *kāhuna*. She is the seventh woman in the family to have served in this capacity, which is usually reserved for men. She says she lifted the *kapu* (taboo) on the *heiau* in 1978 to make it "... safe for the people to come in and go out without harm." Located on a three-acre parcel of land, Mo'okini Heiau was the first site in Hawai'i to be designated a National Historic Landmark, according to the Historic Sites Act of 1935. Stabilized with state funds, it is now a part of Lapakahi State Historical Park, with the provision that it not be excavated. Mo'okini Luakini Inc., a nonprofit foundation, was established to help care for and preserve the complex. For more information, write to Mrs. Leimomi Mo'okini Lum, P.O. Box 7125, Honolulu, HI 96821, or to Lapakahi State Historical Park, P.O. Box 100, Kapa'au, HI 96755 (Tel: 889-5566). (1/94-95; 10/33-34; 11/392-395; 14/58; 16/160; 37/157-58; 43/173-178)

> *Na ka pō i kūkulu a'e iā Mo'okini,*
> *a na Pa'ao na'e.*
> Night built the temple of Mo'okini, for Pa'ao.
> *(Unseen help comes to the favored.)*
> —Hawaiian saying (18/37)

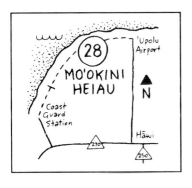

V.28~LOCATION: Outside Hāwī town, off Akoni Pule Highway 270. Take the secondary road two miles to 'Upolu Airport and continue 1.6 miles to the left until the *hciau* appears on the *ma uka* (toward the mountains) side of the road.

## V.29 Kamehameha Rock
Pōhaku

Easily found along the side of the road, Kamehameha Rock is a *pōhaku* (stone) said to have come to the Big Island all the way from the sacred Waialua district on Kaua'i in a double-hulled canoe. The reason for its journey is not known. It was said that only high-ranking *ali'i* (chiefs) could move it; Kamehameha I not only moved it but he is said to have carried the stone from the ocean to its present resting place. Note the similar story attached to the Pinao Pōhaku (Site I.4, pg. 53). Lifting heavy stones was not only a sign of strength in ancient Hawai'i, it was also a form of exercise as can be seen by the lifting stones, similar to cannon balls, used by *ali'i*. An example of these can be found at Hulihe'e Palace in Kailua-Kona.

A Hawaiʻi Visitors Bureau sign marks the spot where the legendary Kamehameha Rock lies. (44/73)

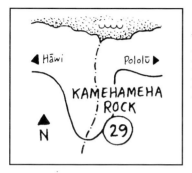

V.29~LOCATION: 4.3 miles east of Hāwī center, on Route 270, near Hālawa. Marked by a Hawaiʻi Visitors Bureau sign.

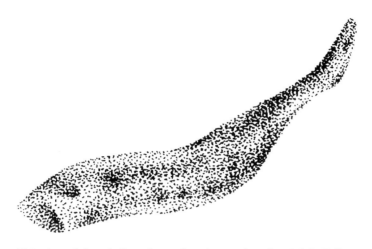

This stone fish god, three feet in length, was found in Pololū Valley, North Kohala, not far from the Kamehameha Rock, and now rests in the courtyard at Bishop Museum.

Shrine at Mauna Kea Adz Quarry. (Photograph courtesy Bishop Museum Department of Anthropology)

## VI  Hāmākua

Hāmākua district was known as *kihi loa*, the "long corner," because it stretches from the oldest valleys on the northern coast to the far northwest summit of Mauna Loa, touching every other land section on the island with the exception of Puna. It also has within its borders the highest elevation in the state, Mauna Kea (White Mountain), at 13,796 feet.

Near the summit of this mountain is Mauna Kea Ice Age Natural Area Reserve, which includes an ancient adze quarry at Keanakākoʻi (the adze-making cave) Crater, where stone tools once were fashioned. What is probably the largest and densest flow of hard blue-black basalt in the islands was formed here when a volcanic eruption was quick-cooled by the glacial ice that once capped Mauna Kea. The flow provided an exceptional resource for the making of adze heads. The adze was an important cutting tool, similar to an axe and a chisel, used by Hawaiians for a multitude of purposes. Archaeologists suggest that adzes from this source were used beyond Hawaiʻi Island and radiocarbon dates indicate that the Mauna Kea site was in full use  well before the fifteenth century. This site is not accessible to the public.

Much of  Hāmākua has been utilized for the cultivation of sugar cane during the twentieth century. This and the fact that little archaeological work has been carried out here gives us few ancient sites to visit in this region. In fact, the only site listed here is the north shore valley of Waipiʻo, which is perhaps a fitting conclusion to this overview of ancient sites of Hawaiʻi Island. Waipiʻo Valley demonstrates how the land itself with all its natural features—waterfalls, streams, ponds, bays, valley walls, rock formations, and flora—is an ancient, yet contemporary, site and a sacred place. The taro patches, fishponds, rock walls, shrines, and *heiau* serve as focal points to connect the human being, on the one hand, to the earth and nature, and, on the other, to the gods. In this sense the entire valley can be seen as a self-contained and complete world unto itself, a self-sustaining ecosystem as so many other places in Hawai'i once were. The natural world and the spirit of old Hawai'i come together in a very special way in Waipi'o Valley, which is still mostly unspoiled and relatively un-affected by modern times.

Waipi'o Valley is majestic, powerful, and silent. It still seems to possess the secrets of its ancient past. We of the present and the future must not be deaf to the quiet message of Waipi'o, and the *wahi pana* of Hawai'i Island.

> *Hāmākua 'āina pali loa.*
> Hāmākua, land of tall cliffs.
>
> *(Praise of Hāmākua, Hawai'i.)*
> —Hawaiian saying (35/53)

# Hāmākua Region sites

### 30. Waipiʻo Valley

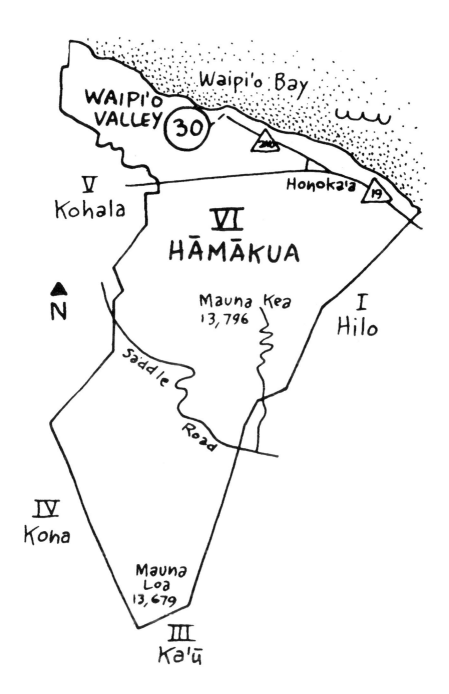

## VI.30 ~ Waipi'o Valley
*North shore valley and natural features*

Waipi'o Valley is the largest, oldest, and perhaps most beautiful of Hawai'i Island's valleys. It is one mile wide at the shoreline and six miles long. A spectacular double waterfall, Hi'ilawe, which means "lift [and] carry," is the tallest in the state with a vertical drop of more than 1,000 feet. Waipi'o is a rich agricultural valley, to this day producing taro, banana, and other wetland crops typical of old Hawai'i. Waipi'o is also rich in history, having been the home of ancient Hawaiians who built fishponds, *heiau* (temples) and a *pu'uhonua* (place of refuge) within the valley

It is said that an entranceway into the underworld, whereby souls left the land of the living, could be found in Waipi'o Valley. However, the story says that this was lost after a sugar company plowed part of the valley.

According to oral tradition, the soil of the upper valley is red because the god Kanaloa threw the demigod Māui down on the earth so hard that he bled all over the ground. It is also said that a cruel chief in ancient times reddened the earth by sacrificing eighty people at a Waipi'o valley *luakini heiau* (temple of human sacrifice).

Pāka'alana Pu'uhonua was a place of refuge for *kapu* (taboo) breakers in the valley. It was located 300 feet inland on the west side of the valley and was built before the time of Kila, more than 600 years ago. Directly on the beach was Honua'ula Heiau, of the *luakini* type, built by chief Līloa and dedicated to the god Kā'ili. A tunnel is said to have connected the *heiau* with the *pu'uhonua*. Honua'ula Heiau measured more than 210 feet by more than 90 feet before a 1946 tsunami destroyed the structure. Other temples in Waipi'o were Moa'ula Heiau at the base of the northwest valley wall, 2,500 feet from the ocean, built by chief Hākau but dedicated by chief 'Umi, who killed Hākau and used his body as the offering; Kuahailo Heiau on the west side of the valley, 7,000 feet from the sea, and built to honor the god Kuahailo, who was believed to reside in a cave near the top of the south cliff; Hōkūwelowelo Heiau, said to have been "built by the gods," at the mouth of Waipi'o Valley; and Palaka Heiau, an enclosure at Waiamoa. It is said that when the *kapu* were broken in 1819 by Kamehameha II, only Hale o Keawe Heiau in Hōnaunau and a Hale o Lono temple at Waipi'o were spared. Two *heiau* foundations still exist on private property in Waipi'o Valley.

Close to the beach is a *loko pu'uone*, a fishpond fed by streams and springs and separated from the ocean by a sand dune, called Lālākea. Meaning "white fin," Lālākea is also the Hawaiian name for the whitetip shark.

Kamehameha the Great spent much of his youth in Waipi'o Valley, and in 1780 received his commission from the paramount chief of Hawai'i Island to be the guardian of the war god, Kūkā'ilimoku. According to tradition, it was this god who eventually gave him the power to conquer his enemies and unite all of the Hawaiian Islands.

Waipi'o means "curved water," and its mile-wide black sand beach and good surf attracted *ali'i* to test their wave-riding skills in ancient times. Just offshore, in 1791, Kamehameha I engaged the attacking forces of Kahekili, from Maui, in the first Hawaiian naval battle to use cannon. The battle, which was not decisive for either side, was called Kepūwaha'ula'ula, "red-mouthed cannon."

From a lookout above the valley, a mile-long descent along a narrow paved road leads to the valley floor. There are only dirt roads in the valley, many of them crisscrossed by streams. A four-wheel-drive vehicle is a must if you intend to drive, but the best way to see Waipi'o is certainly on foot. There are also several different tours of the valley that one can purchase. Choose from horseback tours, mule-drawn wagon rides, and four-wheel-drive shuttles. Arrangements can be made through most travel agents. There are even a small rustic hotel and a bed-and-breakfast if overnight accommodations are desired. Please remember to treat Waipi'o Valley with the same care and respect you would give to any ancient site of Hawai'i.    (1/94-95; 11/355-368; 14/19; 37/227; 43/159-163; 44/66-69)

> *He he'e hōlua.*
> One who rides a *hōlua* sled.
>
> *(Said proudly of being a descendant of the chiefly families of Waipi'o, Hawai'i, who were well known for their skill in hōlua sledding.)*
> —Hawaiian saying (35/66)

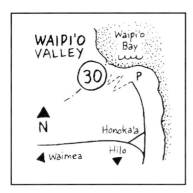

VI.30~LOCATION: At the end of Route 240 out of Honoka'a.

# APPENDIX A

## Selected Sites for Visitors

Most visitors to Hawai'i will find themselves staying in either Hilo or Kona, probably for a few days. The Hilo guest can certainly see all the ancient sites listed in this region within the course of a day and all the sites in the Puna district on another day. The visitor staying in Kona or along the Kohala Coast would require several days, at least, to visit adequately that region's ancient sites. However, visitors to both Hilo and Kona sides of the island may wish to strike out to other parts of the island and may have only a limited time to visit ancient sites. Therefore, the following twelve sites are recommended as most essential for experiencing Hawai'i Island's ancient historical resources.

In Hilo, one should not miss Rainbow Falls (Site I.3, pg. 51), one of the most beautiful and most photographed waterfalls in Hawai'i, and 'Akaka Falls (Site I.1, pg. 47) fifteen miles north of town. Although both are standard tourist stops, they nevertheless maintain their spectacular natural beauty and legendary splendor.

If you are visiting the Hawai'i Volcanoes National Park in the Puna district and you decide to take the fifty-mile round-trip Chain of Craters Road to the coast pull-over, park the car and stretch your legs by walking the ancient trail to the famous Pu'u Loa Petroglyphs (Site II.9, pg. 66).

The Punalu'u Fishpond (Site III.12, pg. 77) in the Ka'ū district is just off the Hawai'i Belt Road and certainly worth a visit on the drive to Kona. A swim at the Punalu'u Black Sand Beach and lunch at the Punalu'u Restaurant are a pleasant complement to viewing the ancient sites in the area.

Once you enter the Kona district, Pu'uhonua o Hōnaunau is a must-see site (Site IV.14, pg. 89), and not far away is the historic site of Captain James Cook's landing and Hikiau Heiau (Site IV.15, pg.94).

In Kohala, visitors should try to see the Waikoloa Petroglyph Preserve at 'Anaeho'omalu (Site V.22, pg. 120), Kalāhuipua'a (Site V.23, pg. 126), Puakō Petroglyphs (Site V.24, pg. 130), Pu'ukoholā Heiau (Site V.25, pg. 133), Lapakahi State Historical Park (Site V.26, pg. 139), and Mo'okini Heiau (Site V.28, pg. 139).

Waipi'o Valley (Site VI.30, pg. 152) in the Hāmākua district is also a highly recommended point of interest for visitors seeking the natural beauty as it must have been in ancient Hawai'i.

Petroglyphs were still being carved in the early historic period as can be seen by this European ship at Kapalaoa, Kona.

# APPENDIX B

## Collections and Cultural Events

Local museums have collected many artifacts and assembled a good deal of research concerning the ancient sites of Hawai'i, the entire archipelago, and the whole of the Pacific region. The Bishop Museum, located in Honolulu, has the most extensive collection of Pacific Island material in the world. In addition to its artifacts, this museum has an extensive research library, and its scientific and cultural departments sponsor numerous lectures, classes, and educational activities.

> Bishop Museum
> 1525 Bernice St.
> Honolulu, Hawai'i
> (808) 848-4129 or 847-3511
> Hours: Daily, 9 A.M. to 5 P.M.
> Admission fee

On the Big Island, the best collections of ancient artifacts can be found at the Lyman Museum in Hilo, Hulihe'e Palace in Kailua-Kona, and the Kamuela Museum in Waimea.

> Lyman House Memorial Museum
> 276 Hili Street
> Hilo, Hawai'i
> (808) 935-5021
> Hours: Monday through Saturday,
>     10 A.M. to 4 P.M.
> Admission fee

> Hulihe'e Palace
> 75-5718 Ali'i Drive
> Kailua-Kona, Hawai'i
> (808) 329-1877
> Hours: Daily, 9 A.M. to 4 P.M.
> Admission fee

Kamuela Museum
Junction of Hwys. 25 and 19
Waimea, Hawai'i
(808) 885-4724
Hours: Daily, 10 A.M. to 5 P.M.
Admission fee

The Kona Historical Society and Museum in Kealakekua town has a small collection of mostly historic artifacts (due to irregular hours, call Tel: 329-1877), and a number of resorts such as the King Kamehameha Hotel in Kona, the Royal Waikoloan in Kohala, and the Mauna Lani Resort in Kohala, have exhibits of replica artifacts.

Every April, Hilo's Kanaka'ole Stadium is the site of the renowned Merrie Monarch Festival. This outstanding Hawaiian dance competition celebrates the art of both ancient and modern *hula* presented by some of the best *hālau* (schools or groups) in the islands. (Tel: 935-9168)

Hawaiian cultural festivals are also held annually at Pu'ukoholā National Historic Site in North Kohala. For exact dates on these and other National Parks programs, contact the National Parks Service (Tel: 967-7311) in Hawai'i.

Some organizations promoting the preservation and appreciation of ancient sites in Hawai'i are:

Historic Sites Section
Department of Land and Natural Resources
State of Hawai'i
P.O. Box 621
Honolulu, HI 96809

Rock Art Association of Hawai'i
P.O. Box 37902
Honolulu, HI 96837

Society for Hawaiian Archaeology
P.O. Box 23292
Honolulu, HI 96823

# APPENDIX C

## Preservation

The ancient sites of Hawai'i are cultural treasures and as such are invaluable to all people, of all ethnic backgrounds, for all time. They provide spiritual inspiration as well as irreplaceable knowledge. The archaeological resources of all the Hawaiian Islands need to be protected against natural destructive forces as well as careless individuals and groups seeking short-term gain.

Since the Antiquities Act of 1906, numerous federal laws have been passed by the United States Congress to help protect and conserve the ancient sites located on public lands and reservations throughout America. The National Historic Preservation Act of 1966 is a particularly effective piece of legislation in this regard. As a result of such legislation, many sites have been listed on the national and state registers in order to secure official recognition of their significance as historic places and to aid in their preservation. Oddly enough, actual protection is not guaranteed these sites unless they fall within special county-zoned districts or state conservation areas.

None of the federal laws, nor similar state laws, can protect all sites, especially those on private property where landowners may knowingly or unknowingly destroy important contextual evidence as well as valuable artifacts. Hawai'i State law requires site surveys of both public and private lands slated for development, but because the developer hires the archaeologist, a conflict of interest may arise, even if only in theory. Therefore, even with the survey reviews provided by the State Historic Preservation Division of the Department of Land and Natural Resources, weak links in the preservation process can occur.

Public interest and understanding are necessary for any law to be truly effective. Each citizen has a role to play and must take at least partial responsibility for the preservation of ancient sites. Only through vocal support and local action can historic and prehistoric sites be protected from not only natural deterioration but also vandalism and the rapid, sometimes thoughtless, land development of the kind that has already devastated an estimated two-thirds of the known ancient sites on O'ahu.

To combat further destruction of ancient Hawaiian sites, tour the accessible sites and educate yourself and others about them so that you and your family gain an understanding of the importance of such places. When you see preliminary signs of land-use change or development, ask the land owner (or the state) if the site has been surveyed by archaeologists. And, as the National Park Service recommends, when visiting an ancient site, take nothing but photographs and leave nothing but footprints.

An anchor petroglyph at 'Anaeho'omalu may indicate the value placed on metal objects by Hawaiians of the early historic period. It may also be a sign of conversion to the new religion brought to the islands by missionaries, beginning in 1820. From early Christian times the anchor has been a symbol of firm belief, unswerving faith, and religious hope.

# APPENDIX D

## Hawaiian Pronunciation

Hawaiian is a lovely, melodious language. The alphabet, developed with the help of missionaries from the oral language of ancient Hawai'i, comprises thirteen letters: These are seven consonants, **h, k, l, m,n, p, w,** as well as the 'okina (see below), and five vowels, **a, e, i, o, u.**

Pronunciation of the consonants is roughly similar to that of their English counterparts. The letter **w** is the most different, usually pronounced like a **v** after **i** and **e**, and like a **w** after **u** and **o.** When **w** is the first letter, it can be pronounced either **v** or **w.**

All words end in a vowel and vowels are generously used, sometimes in surprising combinations by comparison to English usage. Many words consist solely of vowel clusters. Thus, the following sentence becomes possible in Hawaiian: *I 'Aiea i 'ai 'ia ai ia i'a.* (In [the town of] 'Aiea the aforementioned fish was eaten.)

Hawaiian vowels are generally pronounced as their equivalents in Spanish or Japanese. However, with the addition of a glottal stop, called an *'okina* (written as an inverted apostrophe in front of a vowel: **'a**), or a macron, called a *kahakō* (written as a horizontal line over a vowel: **ā**), the sound quality of the vowel changes. Many Hawaiian language specialists consider the *'okina* to be the eighth consonant.

The glottal stop is common in many Polynesian languages. It can be described as a momentary stoppage of the air flow passing through the glottis, producing a sudden small thrust of air not unlike a tiny cough. The closest equivalent in English might be the catch of air in the utterance of "Oh-oh!" when something is amiss.

The macron doubles the sound length of a vowel.

The proper use of the glottal stop and the macron is critical to correct pronunciation of Hawaiian words. Many words whose letter spelling is the same have very different meanings depending on the presence or absence of these two marks:

| | |
|---|---|
| kau | to place, put, hang |
| kāu | your, yours |
| ka'u | my, mine |
| Ka'ū | name of a district on the island of Hawai'i |

Diacritical markings in the text have been used in accordance with contemporary usage as predicated on recommendations of 'Ahahui 'Ōlelo Hawai'i (1978) and the Pukui-Elbert *Hawaiian Dictionary* (1986). However, the numerous references and quotes in this book taken from ' Ōlelo No'eau, *Hawaiian Proverbs & Poetical Sayings*, by Mary Kawena Pukui, retain the original orthography that reflects an older practice.

Determining the proper use of diacritical markings in place names can be particularly challenging. The standard reference work on this subject is *Place Names of Hawai'i* (1981). Unfortunately, many locations are not listed in that book. Important areas are well known and easily recognizable; other more remote locations, however, have been lost to lava, to bulldozers, or to our memory. In the absence of an unbroken oral tradition (Hawaiian was actively suppressed following the overthrow of the monarchy in 1893), the pronunciation as well as the meaning of many words has also vanished or been distorted. This book follows current practice in the use of diacritical markings: Place names whose pronunciation cannot be verified have been left unmarked.

—David L. Eyre
Hawaiian Language Instructor
Kamehameha Schools

Names and dates carved in Roman-style lettering taught to the Hawaiians by missionaries before 1870 can be found at various petroglyph sites including this one in the Waikoloa Petroglyph Preserve at 'Anaeho'omalu, Kohala.

# GLOSSARY OF TERMS

**a'ā.** Rough, clinker lava.

**āholehole.** Young endemic flagtail fish used for magic.

**ahu.** Heap of stones.

**ahupua'a.** Land division.

**akua.** God, goddess, image, idol, spirit.

**akua ki'i.** Image representing a god.

**ala.** Path, way, or trail.

**'alā.** Smooth, waterworn lava stones.

**ali'i.** Chief, chiefess, king, queen, royalty, nobility.

**aloha.** Hello, goodbye, warm greeting, love.

**'ama'ama.** Young mullet fish.

**'anae.** Full-sized *'ama'ama* mullet fish.

**'anu'u.** Ancient *heiau* tower.

**'Āpa'apa'a.** Strong North Kohala wind.

**'apukōheoheo.** Deadly poison given to *kapu* breakers.

**'aumakua.** Ancestral spirit or personal god. (Pl.) *'aumākua.*

**awa.** Milkfish.

**'awa.** Plant root used to make a narcotic drink.

**haku mele.** Poet, one who composes a chant.

**hālau.** School, training, group.

**hale.** House, building, home place.

**hale mana.** Large house in a *luakini* temple.

**hale noa.** House where entire family could meet without
   *kapu.*

**Hale o Lono.** Temples dedicated to Lono, god of agriculture.

**hale pahu.** Drum house.

**Hāmākua.** Land district on island of Hawai'i.

**Hawai'i.** The island group as a state; also, the largest and
   most recently formed island of the group, also called
   the Big Island.

**heiau.** Hawaiian temple, place of worship or offering; stone
   platform or earth terrace.

**heiau ho'oulu 'ai.** Temple devoted to increase of food

supply.

**heiau ma'o.** Temple to promote rainfall.

**hilo.** Twisting, braiding. (Cap.) Town and district of Hawai'i Island.

**holehole.** To peel, to strip off.

**hōlua.** Ancient Hawaiian sport, sled course, slide.

**Honolulu.** "Sheltered bay." Capital city of the State of Hawai'i on the island of O'ahu.

**ho'okupu.** Gifts, sprout.

**ho'omalu.** Protection, reserved, taboo.

**hula.** Ancient art of dance.

**'ie'ie.** Vine growing in high country.

**'ili'ili.** Pebble, small rock. Used as *hula* stones.

**ka'ao.** Fanciful tale.

**kaha ki'i.** Scratched or drawn images.

**kahakō.** Macron.

**Kahiki.** Anyplace "abroad." Legendary island home of the ancient Hawaiians; thought by some to be Tahiti.

**Kaho'olawe.** Name of one of the Hawaiian islands.

**kahuna.** Priest, shaman, expert, master. (Pl.) kāhuna.

**kahuna hana 'upena.** Master fishnetmaker.

**kahuna ho'okele.** Navigator.

**kahuna ho'oulu 'ai.** Agricultural expert.

**kahuna kālai.** Carving expert, sculptor.

**kahuna kuhikuhipu'uone.** Architect.

**kahuna lapa'au.** Medical practitioner, healer.

**kahuna nui.** High priest.

**kai.** Sea water, salt water.

**kākū.** Barracuda.

**kalo.** Taro.

**kama'āina.** Child of the land, native-born, familiar; now commonly used to mean long-time resident.

**Kamehameha.** Name of a line of Hawai'i Island chiefs/ monarchs.

**Kanaloa.** God of the oceans.

**kāne.** Man, male, husband. (Cap.) God of fresh water sources.

**kapa.** Tapa, barkcloth.

**kapu.** Taboo, forbidden, sacred, consecrated.

**Ka'ū.** Land district on the island of Hawai'i.

**kauā.** Outcast person.

**Kaua'i.** Name of one of the Hawaiian islands.

**kāula.**  Seer, prophet.

**kepie.**  Sled used in *hōlua* racing.

**kī.**  Tī, a woody plant of the lily family whose leaves are often used in rituals, as well as in everyday life.

**kihi loa.**  Means the "long corner" and refers to the Hāmākua district on the Big Island.

**ki'i.**  Image, statue, picture.

**ki'i pōhaku.**  Petroglyphs, images carved in stone.

**koa.**  Largest of the native forest trees, warrior, brave.

**ko'a.**  Fishing shrine; coral; coral head; fishing grounds.

**Kohala.**  Land district on island of Hawai'i.

**Kona.**  Leeward sides of the Hawaiian Islands; district on Hawai'i Island.

**kōnane.**  Ancient game resembling checkers.

**konohiki.**  Overseer of land and fishing rights.

**Ko'olau.**  Windward sides of the Hawaiian Islands.

**kū.**  To stand; stop. (Cap.) God of war.

**kuapā.**  Fishpond walls.

**kuhina nui.**  Prime minister.

**kupua.**  Spirit being that can change its shape from one form into another.

**kū'ula.**  Altar or stone used to worship or attract fish or fishgods.

**Lāna'i.**  Name of one of the Hawaiian islands.

**lapa'au.**  Medical practice; to heal, cure.

**lei.**  Flower garland.

**lele.**  An altar, offering stand.

**limu.**  General name for underwater plants, seaweed.

**loko.**  Pond or fishpond.

**loko pu'uone.**  Fishpond separated from the ocean by a sand dune and fed by streams, springs, or both.

**Lono.**  God of agriculture, peace, and Makahiki.

**lua.**  Pit, indentation, hole.

**luakini.**  Hawaiian temple where ruling chiefs prayed and human sacrifices were offered.

**luapa'ū.**  Refuse pit found at *luakini heiau*.

**maile.**  Native twining shrub.

**mākāhā.**  Sluice gates used in fishponds.

**malihini.**  Newcomer, of foreign origin.

**Makahiki.**  (Cap.) Ancient festival beginning about mid-October and lasting four months.  Sport and religious festivities were conducted at this time and war was *kapu.*

**makai.** Towards the ocean.

**mana.** Spiritual, divine, or miraculous power.

**Mānaiakalani.** Ceremonial hook used to pierce the mouth of a human sacrifice.

**manini.** Common reef surgeonfish.

**Maui.** Name of one of the Hawaiian Islands.

**Māui.** Name of a demigod.

**mauka.** Towards the mountains.

**menehune.** Legendary race of small people who worked at night during prehistoric times building temples, roads, fishponds, and other structures.

**moa pahe'e.** Dart sliding game.

**mō'ī.** High chief, king.

**Moloka'i.** Name of one of the Hawaiian Islands.

**mo'o.** Lizard, reptile, dragon, serpent.

**mo'olelo.** Myth, tradition, history.

**O'ahu.** One of the Hawaiian Islands.

**ōhi'a.** Two kinds of trees, the mountain apple and the lehua blossom bearer.

**'okina.** Glottal stop.

**'ōpae'oeha'a.** Clawed shrimp.

**ōpū.** Temple tower.

**ō'ō.** Endemic bird to Hawai'i, now extinct.

**ō'ō ihe.** Spear throwing.

**'o'opu.** Gobies, a fish.

**Pā'ao.** Traditional tenth-to-thirteenth-century *kahuna* believed to have brought a colony to Hawai'i from the South Pacific, possibly Tahiti. Said to have introduced human sacrifice.

**pāhoehoe.** Smooth or ropy lava.

**pahu.** Drum.

**pala'ie.** Loop and ball game.

**pali.** Cliff, precipice.

**paniolo.** Cowboy.

**pāpio.** Young *ulua* fish.

**pele.** Volcano, lava. (Cap.) Volcano goddess.

**piko.** Umbilical cord stump.

**pili.** A grass used for thatching.

**Pō.** The realm of the gods, night, darkness.

**pōhaku.** Rock, stone.

**Pōhaku o Kane.** Sacred stone.

**pono.** Righteous, upright, moral.

**pua'a.** Pig or boar.

**pua'a kai.** " Sea pigs," referring to mullet fish.

**puhi.** Moray eel.

**puka.** Hole or opening; also, to proclaim or speak.

**Puna.** Land district on the island of Hawai'i.

**pu'u.** Any kind of protuberance, bulge, heap, pile, mound, hill, peak.

**pu'uhonua.** Place of refuge, sanctuary.

**tapa.** (See *kapa.*)

**taro.** (See *kalo.*)

**ti.** (See *kī.*)

**tsunami.** Tidal wave (Japanese).

**ulua.** Jackfish.

**'ulu maika.** A disk rolling game.

**'umeke.** Calabash.

**wa'a.** Dugout canoe.

**wahi pana.** Sacredness of place.

**wai.** Fresh water; any liquid other than sea water.

**wai ea.** A small thatched house within the temple precinct where incantations were invoked.

Human figure with circle and dot symbols at Pu'uloa.

# BIBLIOGRAPHY

1.  Armstrong, R. W., *et al.*  1973.  *Atlas of Hawaii*, 2nd ed. Honolulu: University of Hawaii Press.

2.  Barrere, W., and M. Kelly.  1974.  *Archaeological and Historical Survey of the Waimea to Kawaihae Road Corridor, Island of Hawaii*. Honolulu:  Bishop Museum Press.

3.  Barrere, D. B. 1975.  *Kamehameha in Kona: Two Documentary Studies.*  Pacific Anthropological Records No. 23.  Honolulu: Bishop Museum Press .

4.  Bevacqua, R. F., and T. S. Dye.  1972.  *Archaeological Reconnaissance of Proposed Kapoho-Kalapana Highway, District of Puna, Island of Hawaii.*  Honolulu: Bishop Museum Press (BPBM).

5.  Bryan, E. H., and K. P. Emory.  1986.  *The Natural and Cultural History of Hōnaunau, Kona, Hawai'i.*  Honolulu:  Bishop Museum Press (BPBM).

6.  Ching, F. K. W.  1971.  *Hawaii State Archaeological Journal 71-1:  The Archaeology of South Kohala and North Kona.*  Honolulu:  Department of Land and Natural Resources, State of Hawaii.

7.  Cluff, D. F., W. K. Kikuchi, *et al.*  1969.  *The Archaeological Surface Survey of Puu Kohola Heiau and Mailekini Heiau, South Kohala, Kawaihae, Hawaii Island.*  Honolulu:  Hawaii State Archaeological Journal 69-3.

8.  Cox, J. H., and E. Stasack.  1970.  *Hawaiian Petroglyphs.*  Honolulu: Bishop Museum Press.

9. Dale, P. W. 1969. *Seventy North to Fifty South: Captain Cook's Last Voyage.* Englewood, N.J.: Prentice-Hall.

10. Division of Parks, Outdoor Recreation and Historic Sites. 1972. *North Kohala Preservation of Historical Resources.* Honolulu: Department of Land and Natural Resources, State of Hawaii.

11. Ellis, W. 1969. *Polynesian Researches: Hawaii.* Japan: Charles E. Tuttle Company.

12. Emory, K. P., P. C. McCoy, and D. B. Barrere. 1971. *Archaeological Survey: Kahaluu and Keauhou, North Kona, Hawaii.* Honolulu: Bishop Museum Press (BPBM).

13. Emory, K. P., and L. J. Soehren. 1971. *Archaeological and Historical Survey Honokohau Area, North Kona, Hawaii.* Honolulu: Bishop Museum Press (BPBM).

14. Hagman, M. 1988. *Hawaii Parklands: An Interpretive Companion to Hawaii's National, State, County and Private Parks.* Billings, Montana: Falcon Press Pub. Co. Inc.

15. Hiroa, T. R. (Buck, P. H.). 1988. *Arts and Crafts of Hawaii: XI Religion.* Honolulu: Bishop Museum Press.

16. I'i, J. P. 1983. *Fragments of Hawaiian History.* Special Publication 70. Honolulu: Bishop Museum Press.

17. James, V. 1991. *Ancient Sites of O'ahu: A Guide to Hawaiian Archaeological Places of Interest.* Honolulu: Bishop Museum Press.

18. Judd, H. P. 1930. *Hawaiian Proverbs and Riddles.* Honolulu: Bishop Museum (Bulletin 77).

19. Kalakaua, D. 1990. *The Legends and Myths of Hawaii.* Honolulu. Mutual Publishing.

20. Kamakau, S. M. 1976. *The Works of the People of Old.* Honolulu: Bishop Museum Press.

21. Kelly, M. 1969. *Historical Background of the South Point Area.* Pacific Anthropological Records #6. Honolulu: Bishop Museum Press.

22. Kelly, M. 1971. *Kekaha: 'Aina Malo'o: Historical Survey and Background of Kaloko and Kuki'o Ahupua'a, North Kona, Hawaii.* Honolulu: Bishop Museum Press (BPBM).

23. Kelly, M. 1980. *Majestic Ka'ū: Mo'olelo of Nine Ahupua'a.* Honolulu: Bishop Museum Press.

24. Kelly, M. 1983. *Nā Māla o Kona: Gardens of Kona.* Honolulu: Bishop Museum Press.

25. Kelly, M., B. Nakamura, and D. B. Barrere. 1981. *Hilo Bay: A Chronological History.* Honolulu: Bishop Museum Press.

26. Kirch, P. V. 1985. *Feathered Gods and Fishhooks.* Honolulu: University of Hawaii Press.

27. Kwiatkowski, P. F. 1991. *Na Ki'i Pōhaku: A Hawaiian Petroglyph Primer.* Honolulu: Ku Pa'a Inc.

28. Ladefoged, T., *et al.* 1987. *A Settlement Pattern Analysis of a Portion of Hawaii Volcanoes National Park.* Western Archaeological and Conservation Center, Publications in Anthropology #44.

29. Lee, P., and K. Willis. 1987. *Tales of the Night Rainbow.* Honolulu: Paia-Kapela-Willis 'Ohana, Inc.

30. Malo, D. 1971. *Hawaiian Antiquities (Mo'olelo Hawai'i).* 2nd ed. Honolulu: Bishop Museum Press.

31. Masse, W. B., L. A. Carter, and G. F. Somers. 1991. *"Waha'ula Heiau: The Regional and Symbolic Context of Hawai'i Island's 'Red Mouth' Temple."* Asian Perspectives, vol. 30, no. 1. Honolulu: University of Hawaii Press.

32. McBride, L. R. 1969. *Petroglyphs of Hawaii.* Hilo: Petroglyph Press.

33. Newman, T. S., *et al.* 1968. *The Archaeology of North Kohala: Excavations at Lapakahi—Selected Papers.* Honolulu: Hawaii State Archaeological Journal, 69-2.

34. Pearson, R. 1969. *Archaeology on the Island of Hawaii.* Honolulu: Social Science Research Institute, Asian and Pacific Archaeology Series #6.

35. Pukui, M. K. 1983. *'Ōlelo No'eau: Hawaiian Proverbs and Poetical Sayings.* Honolulu: Bishop Museum Press.

36. Pukui, M. K., and S. H. Elbert. 1986. *Hawaiian Dictionary.* Honolulu: University of Hawaii Press.

37. Pukui, M. K., S. H. Elbert, and E. T. Mookini. 1966. *Place Names of Hawaii.* Honolulu: University of Hawaii Press.

38. Reed, F. 1987. *Hilo Legends.* Hilo: Petroglyph Press.

39. Renger, R. C. 1970. *Archaeological Surface Survey of the Coastal Areas of Kaloko and Kukio, North Kona, Hawaii.* Honolulu: Bishop Museum Press.

40. Rice, W. H. 1923. *Hawaiian Legends.* Honolulu: Bishop Museum Press.

41. Rosendahl, P. H., and M. A. Kelly. 1973. *Archaeological Salvage of the Keahole to Anaehoomalu Section of the Kailua-Kawaihae Road (Queen Kaahumanu Highway), Island of Hawaii.* Honolulu: Bishop Museum Press (BPBM).

42. Soehren, L. J., & D. P. Tuohy. 1987. *Archaeological Excavations at Pu'uhonua o Hōnaunau National Historic Park, Hōnaunau, Kona, Hawaii.* Honolulu: Bishop Museum Press.

43. Stokes, J. F. G. 1991. *Heiau of the Island of Hawai'i: A Historic Survey of Native Hawaiian Temple Sites.* Honolulu: Bishop Museum Press.

44. Stone, S. C. S. 1988. *The Essential Guide to Hawai'i.* Honolulu: Island Heritage.

45. Summers, C. C. 1964. *Hawaiian Fishponds*. Honolulu: Bishop Museum Press.

46. Valeri, V. 1985. *Kingship and Sacrifice*. Chicago: University of Chicago Press.

47. Vis-Norton, L. W. de. No date. *The Story of the Naha Stone*. Hilo: Board of Trade, Territory of Hawaii.

48. Wyban, C. A. 1992. *Tide and Current: Fishponds of Hawai'i*. Honolulu: University of Hawaii Press.

This petrogly[ph of a profile sitting figure is found at Pu'u Loa, in Puna.